JESUS CHRIST
THE WAY, THE TRUTH, THE LIFE

A daily prayer book

This is a beautiful and exciting prayer book for everyday use. Meditations in words and photographs bring the user into the presence of Christ, the Way, the Truth, the Life.

The first section provides starting points for prayer: texts from scripture and the great spiritual writers, and meditative photographs open the heart to the presence of God. They are woven into themes that cover every aspect of daily life: family, work, faith, forgiveness, anxiety, peace, joy, death . . .

There follow meditations on the mysteries of the Rosary, on the Beatitudes and on the Way of the Cross: here, again, the perspective of scripture opens fresh dimensions in the daily living of the Christian seeking God despite and through his human frailties and preoccupations.

An examination of conscience, based on St Paul's hymn to love in the letter to the Corinthians, concludes the book.

This is a prayer book with a difference. Rooted in scripture, traditional devotions of centuries are brought into the heart of modern life; visual aids to meditation accompany the text, and add a dimension to it. A prayer book to be used every day, and by every kind of person.

The author: David Konstant is Roman Catholic Bishop of Central London. He has wide pastoral experience, and is author of many books, including *A Penitent's Prayer Book, Meeting Christ Now.*

Jesus Christ
the Way, the Truth, the Life

A daily prayer book

DAVID KONSTANT

Collins

Collins Liturgical Publications
187 Piccadilly, London W1V 9DA

First published 1981
ISBN 0 00 599 676 7

Nihil obstat: Anton Cowan
Imprimatur: + Philip Harvey, Bishop in North London
Westminster, 5 January 1981

The Nihil obstat and Imprimatur are a declaration that a book or pamphlet is considered to be free from doctrinal or moral error. It is not implied that those who have granted the Nihil obstat and Imprimatur agree with the contents, opinions, or statements expressed.

Photoset in Great Britain by
Rowland Phototypesetting Ltd, Bury St Edmunds, Suffolk
and printed by
William Collins Sons & Co Ltd, Glasgow

Contents

Introduction

The apostles watched Jesus praying and were so moved by what they saw that they said: 'Lord, teach us to pray.' He said to them,

> 'Say this when you pray:
> Father, may your name be held holy,
> your kingdom come;
> give us each day our daily bread,
> and forgive us our sins,
> for we ourselves forgive each one
> who is in debt to us.
> And do not put us to the test.'

Luke 11: 2–4

Jesus urged his friends to pray: in the privacy of their rooms; together, where a few were assembled in his name; without babbling, but urgently, insistently, with confidence and joy, generously, openly, hopefully, always giving praise to God, and always listening to him. We are his friends, and so we too pray, each in our own way.

Sometimes we may feel the urge to express our prayer in words; at other times we may find that by repeating a word or phrase (like, 'Come, Lord Jesus') we are soon absorbed in God's presence; or perhaps it will be enough for us on occasion to be quite still and know that God enfolds us.

Words, though, are almost always the beginning of our daily prayer. So here are some words that may help us to find God. They are pointers to prayer. Some are the words of the Old Testament psalmist; some are Jesus's own words; some are from the early followers of Jesus; there are prayers hallowed by the Church; and there are words of ordinary people, who in their own way have spoken to God. If they help us in our turn to find God at odd moments of the day, these words have done their work and will not return to him empty handed.

God approaches us through all our senses. So there are many things apart from words that may lead us to prayer. Music, beauty, even something as indefinable as atmosphere, can help us raise our minds and hearts to God. The pictures are chosen with this in view. They may provoke us to prayer, accompany the written word, or stand on their own as a silent meditation on God's work.

The Christian's prayer is focused on Jesus Christ, and the second part of this book reflects on some of his words and actions in the context of our daily lives.

The Rosary is a traditional devotion which invites consideration of a number of the Mysteries of our Lord's life. The meditation on each Mystery is accompanied by an Our Father, ten Hail Mary's and the Glory be to the Father.

The Beatitudes describe the road the Christian is invited to walk. They will speak to different people in different ways, but if we open our hearts to these simple though paradoxical words we will never fail to be refreshed.

The Way of the Cross is another traditional devotion calling us to accompany Christ to Calvary and beyond, to a new and richer life.

We begin our day remembering God's continual

presence, and we end the day trustfully, putting ourselves in his hands. In between times, alone or with others, we may turn to him in adoration, in praise, as petitioners, as sinners. Always we may be sure that he hears and answers our prayers.

The Way, the Truth, the Life

The pattern of this little book of prayers is *Jesus Christ: the Way, the Truth, the Life* – titles of Jesus that inspire unending reflection. Here are three prayers that provide words for meditation.

Come, my Way, my Truth, my Life:
Such a Way as gives us breath:
Such a Truth as ends all strife:
Such a Life as killeth death.

George Herbert

O Lord Jesus Christ, who art the Way, the Truth and the Life, we pray thee suffer us not to stray from thee who art the Way, nor to distrust thee who art the Truth, nor to rest in any other thing than thee, who art the Life. Teach us by thy Holy Spirit what to believe, what to do and wherein to take our rest. Amen.

Erasmus

Lord Jesus Christ, Son of the living God,
teach us to walk in your Way more trustfully,
to accept your Truth more faithfully,
and to share your Life more lovingly.
By the power of the Holy Spirit
help us in our work for the Church
so that we may come as one family
to the kingdom of the Father,
where you live for ever and ever. Amen.

Congress Prayer

Morning Prayer

If we are to remain close to God as to a friend, we need, at certain times of the day, to greet him and to listen to him. When we wake in the morning, and before we go to sleep at night, are good moments to place ourselves in his presence and to be still with him.

The sign of the cross

In the name of the Father,
and of the Son,
and of the Holy Spirit. Amen.

Remember that God is present.

I am here and I call, you will hear me, O God.
Turn your ear to me; hear my words.

Psalm 16 (17): 6

Pause for a moment's silent prayer of adoration.

A prayer of praise and thanks

How great is your name, O Lord our God,
through all the earth!

Your majesty is praised above the heavens;
on the lips of children and of babes

you have found praise to foil your enemy,
to silence the foe and the rebel.

When I see the heavens, the work of your hands,
the moon and the stars which you arranged,
what is man that you should keep him in mind,
mortal man that you care for him?

Yet you have made him little less than a god;
with glory and honour you crowned him,
gave him power over the works of your hand,
put all things under his feet.

All of them, sheep and cattle,
yes, even the savage beasts,
birds of the air, and fish
that make their way through the waters.

How great is your name, O Lord our God,
through all the earth!

Psalm 8

The apostles asked Jesus to teach them to pray; he teaches us the same prayer to God who is our Father:

Our Father, who art in heaven,
hallowed be thy name;
thy kingdom come;
thy will be done on earth as it is in heaven.
Give us this day our daily bread;
and forgive us our trespasses
as we forgive those who trespass against us;
and lead us not into temptation,
but deliver us from evil. Amen.

Pause for a moment's silent reflection; remember those whose forgiveness we need, and those whom we must forgive; remember the blessings that are our daily bread – family, friends, work, leisure, home, happiness – and thank God; remember the hardships and temptations of daily life, and pray for strength and perseverance.

A prayer of self-giving for the day's work

Lord God,
you have brought me to a new day.
Give me grace today to work for your glory,
and for my neighbour's good;
so that all I say and do,
and think and pray,
may make this day a perfect gift. Amen.

A prayer of confidence to the God who always cares

The Lord is my shepherd;
there is nothing I shall want.
Fresh and green are the pastures
where he gives me repose.
Near restful waters he leads me,
to revive my drooping spirit.

He guides me along the right path:
he is true to his name.
If I should walk in the valley of darkness
no evil would I fear.
You are there with your crook and your staff;
with these you give me comfort.

You have prepared a banquet for me
in the sight of my foes.
My head you have anointed with oil;
my cup is overflowing.

Surely goodness and kindness shall follow me
all the days of my life.
In the Lord's own house shall I dwell
for ever and ever.

Psalm 22 (23)

Some prayers for the day

* I praise and thank you, Lord, for your goodness to me.
Stay always close to me.

* Lord, you know me through and through.
Forgive my sins;
give me the grace to choose the better way.

* Lord, I believe in you;
increase my faith.

* Lord, I hope in you;
be a friend to me.

* Lord, I love you;
show me how to live.

We may pause to pray for those we love and those who are in need.

Remember now that we belong to the whole family of God, and ask all the saints to pray for us and with us. Mary is the first of all the saints and so we pray:

Hail Mary, full of grace, the Lord is with thee.
Blessed art thou among women,
and blessed is the fruit of thy womb, Jesus.
Holy Mary, mother of God, pray for us sinners
now and at the hour of our death. Amen.

Finally, as we begin the day's work, we may praise God again in the words of a familiar prayer:

Glory be to the Father,
and to the Son,
and to the Holy Spirit;
as it was in the beginning
is now and ever shall be,
world without end. Amen.

Jesus Christ, the Way

The Lord guides the steps of a man
and makes safe the path of one he loves.
Though he stumble he shall never fall
for the Lord holds him by the hand.
Psalm 36 (37): 23–4

Jesus invites us, like the apostles, to listen to his call and to follow him; to be his disciples; to learn that leadership demands service; to walk the way of self-denial, of poverty and of obedience; to come to him in our sickness, our anger and our sinfulness; to pray; to be unworried; to work confidently and to live peaceably in our homes so as to be happy with him for ever.

VOCATION

God has created me to do him some definite service. He has committed some work to me which he has not committed to another. I have my mission – I may never know it in this life, but I shall be told it in the next.

I am a link in a chain, a bond of connexion between persons. He has not created me for naught. I shall do good, I shall do his work. I shall be an angel of peace, a preacher of truth in my own place while not intending it – if I do but keep his commandments.

Therefore I will trust him. Whatever, wherever I am. I can never be thrown away. If I am in sickness, my

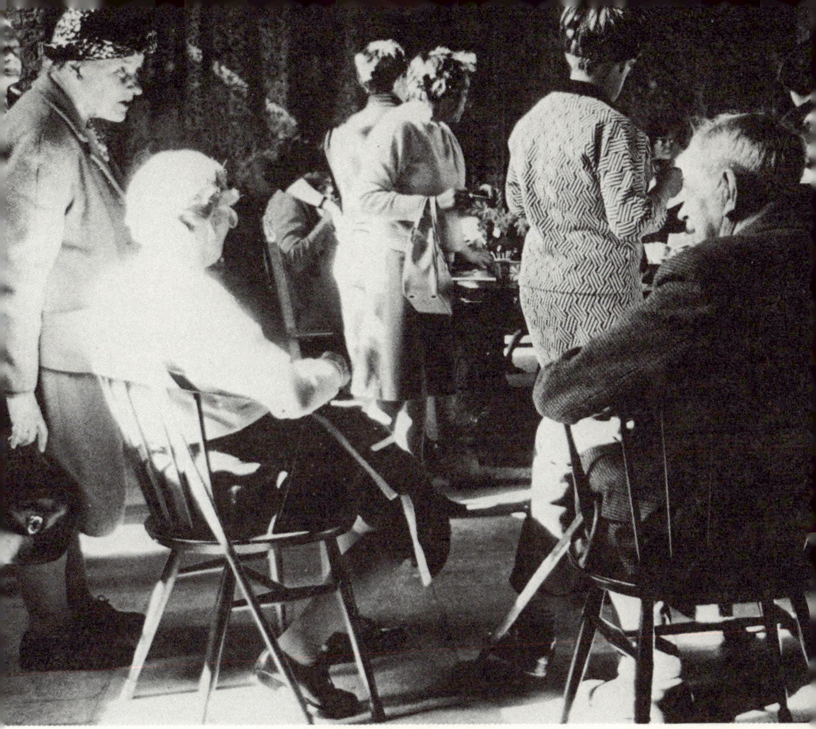

sickness may serve him; in perplexity, my perplexity may serve him; if I am in sorrow, my sorrow may serve him. He does nothing in vain. He knows what he is about. He may take away my friends, he may throw me among strangers. He may make me feel desolate, make my spirits sink, hide my future from me – still he knows what he is about. Cardinal Newman

Lord, give courage and strength to the young. Help them to choose their work and make the right decision for their way of life. Bidding Prayer

Brothers, you have been called and chosen: work all the harder to justify it. In this way you will be granted admittance into the eternal kingdom of our Lord and Saviour Jesus Christ. 2 Peter 1: 10–11

We have been enlightened by Christ.
We are to walk always as children of the light.
May we keep the flame of faith alive in our hearts.
When the Lord comes,
may he go out to meet us with all the saints in the heavenly kingdom.

From the Baptismal Service

DISCIPLESHIP

Christ be near at either hand,
Christ behind, before me stand,
Christ with me where e'er I go,
Christ around, above, below.

Christ be in my heart and mind,
Christ within my soul enshrined,
Christ control my wayward heart;
Christ abide and ne'er depart.

Christ my life and only Way,
Christ my lantern night and day;
Christ be my unchanging friend,
Guide and Shepherd to the end.

tr. J. Fennelly

The Lord says: 'Which is the good way? Take it then, and you shall find rest.' Jeremiah 6: 16

Free your minds, then, of encumbrances; control them, and put your trust in nothing but the grace that will be given you when Jesus Christ is revealed. Do not behave in the way that you liked to before you learnt the truth; make a habit of obedience; be holy in all you do, since it is the Holy One who has called you, and scripture says, 'Be holy, for I am holy'.

1 Peter 1: 13–16

As he was walking on he saw Levi, the son of Alphaeus, sitting by the counting house, and he said to him, 'Follow me'. And he got up and followed him.

Mark 2: 14

Someone said to Jesus, 'I will follow you, sir, but first let me go and say good-bye to my people at home.' Jesus said to him, 'Once the hand is laid on the plough, no one who looks back is fit for the kingdom of God.'

Luke 9: 61–62

'What about us?' Peter asked Jesus, 'We have left everything and followed you.' Jesus said, 'I tell you solemnly, there is no one who has left house, brothers, sisters, father, children or land for my sake and for the sake of the gospel who will not be repaid a hundred times over . . . and in the world to come, eternal life.'

Mark 10: 28–30

Come to me, all you who labour and are overburdened, and I will give you rest. Shoulder my yoke and learn from me, for I am gentle and humble in heart, and you will find rest for your souls. Yes, my yoke is easy, and my burden light. Matthew 11: 28–30

The disciple is not superior to his teacher, nor the slave to his master. It is enough for the disciple that he should grow to be like his teacher, and the slave like his master. Matthew 10: 24–5

In your minds you must be the same as Christ Jesus.

Philippians 2: 5

Lord, I give you today my prayers, thoughts, works, sufferings and joys, that they may be for your glory and for the good of the world. A Morning Offering

Jesu, blessed Jesu, strengthen me in soul and body, that I may not fail you. St John Paine

Jesus said:
'I am the light of the world;
anyone who follows me will not be walking in the dark;
he will have the Light of Life.'

John 8: 12

Lord Jesus,
I give you my hands to do your work.
I give you my feet to go your way.
I give you my eyes to see as you do.
I give you my tongue to speak your words.
I give you my mind that you may think in me.
I give you my spirit that you may pray in me.
Above all, I give you my heart
that you may love in me your Father and all mankind.
I give you my whole self that you may grow in me,
so that it is you, Lord Jesus,
who live and work and pray in me.

Grail Prayer

LEADERSHIP

The greatest among you must be your servant. Anyone who exalts himself will be humbled, and anyone who humbles himself will be exalted. Matthew 23: 11–12

Anyone who wants to become great among you must be your servant, and anyone who wants to be first among you must be slave to all. For the Son of Man himself did not come to be served, but to serve, and to give his life as a ransom for many. Mark 10: 44–5

The Lord carried you as a man carries his child, all along the road you travelled. Deuteronomy 1: 31

Since in Jesus, the Son of God, we have the supreme high priest who has gone through to the highest heaven, we must never let go of the faith that we have professed. For it is not as if we have a high priest who was incapable of feeling our weaknesses with us; but we have one who has been tempted in every way that we are, though he is without sin. Let us be confident, then, in approaching the throne of grace, that we shall have mercy from him and find grace when we are in need of help. Hebrews 4: 15–16

I led you with reins of kindness,
with leading strings of love.

Hosea 11: 3

Let us not lose sight of Jesus, who leads us in our faith and brings it to perfection: for the sake of the joy which was still in the future, he endured the cross, disregarding the shamefulness of it, and from now on has taken his place at the right of God's throne. Hebrews 12: 2

SERVICE

Teach us, good Lord,
to serve you as you deserve;
to give and not to count the cost,
to fight and not to heed the wounds,
to toil and not to seek for rest,
to labour and not to ask for any reward,
save that of knowing that we do your will;
through Jesus Christ our Lord. Amen.

St Ignatius

What does the Lord your God ask of you? Only this: to fear the Lord your God, to follow all his ways, to love him, to serve the Lord your God with all your heart and all your soul. Deuteronomy 10: 12

Repay no one evil for evil. If your enemy is hungry, feed him; if he is thirsty, give him drink. Do not be overcome by evil, but overcome evil with good.

from Romans 12: 17–21

I was hungry and you gave me food.
Blessed be God for ever.
I was thirsty and you gave me drink.
Blessed be God for ever.
I was a stranger and you made me welcome.
Blessed be God for ever.
I was naked and you clothed me.
Blessed be God for ever.
I was sick and you visited me.
Blessed be God for ever.
I was in prison and you came to see me.
Blessed be God for ever.

from Matthew 25

There is a variety of gifts but always the same Spirit; there are all sorts of service to be done, but always to the same Lord; working in all sorts of different ways in different people, it is the same God who is working in all of them. 1 Corinthians 12: 4–6

The greatest among you must behave as if he were the youngest, the leader as if he were the one who serves. For who is the greater: the one at table, or the one who serves? The one at table, surely? Yet here am I among you as one who serves! Luke 22: 27

> I tell you most solemnly,
> no servant is greater than his master,
> no messenger is greater than the man who sent
> him.

John 13: 16

Each one of you has received a special grace, so, like stewards responsible for all these different graces of God, put yourselves at the service of others. If you are a speaker, speak in words that seem to come from God; if you are a helper, help as though every action was done at God's orders; so that in everything God may receive the glory, through Jesus Christ, since to him alone belong all glory and power for ever and ever.

1 Peter 4: 10–11

> Make us worthy, Lord,
> to serve our fellow men throughout the world,
> who live and die in poverty and hunger.
> Give them by our hands
> this day their daily bread,
> and by our understanding love
> give peace and joy.

Pope Paul VI

SELF-DENIAL

Jesus said to his disciples, 'If anyone wants to be a follower of mine, let him renounce himself, and take up his cross and follow me. For anyone who wants to save his life will lose it; but anyone who loses his life for my sake will find it. What, then, will a man gain if he wins the whole world and ruins his life?' Matthew 16: 24–26

Jesus said:

'Unless a grain of wheat falls on the ground and dies,
it remains only a single grain;
but if it dies, it yields a rich harvest.' John 12: 24

He was obedient unto death, even to death on a cross.
Philippians 2: 8

'It makes me happy to suffer for you' writes St Paul, 'as I am suffering now, and in my own body to do what I can to make up all that has still to be undergone by Christ, for the sake of his body, the Church.'
Colossians 1: 24

O blessed Jesu, make me understand and remember that whatsoever we gain, if we lose you, all is lost, and whatsoever we lose, if we gain you, all is gained.
St Thomas Cottam

POVERTY

Happy you who are poor: yours is the kingdom of God.
Alas for you who are rich: you are having your consolation now.

Luke 6: 20, 24

Give your bread to those who are hungry, and your clothes to those who are naked. Whatever you own in plenty, devote a proportion to almsgiving; and when you give alms do not do it grudgingly. Tobit 4: 16–17

O, come to the water all you who are thirsty;
though you have no money, come!
Buy corn without money, and eat,
and, at no cost, wine and milk.

Isaiah 55: 1

O Lord Jesus Christ, take as your right, receive as my gift, all my liberty, my memory, my understanding, my will; all that I have, all that I am, all that I can be. To you, O Lord, I restore it, all is yours, dispose of it according to your will. Give me your love. Give me your grace. It is enough for me. St Ignatius

Jesus was setting out on a journey when a man ran up, knelt before him and put this question to him, 'Good master, what must I do to inherit eternal life?' . . . Jesus looked steadily at him and loved him, and said, 'There is one thing you lack. Go and sell everything you own, and give the money to the poor, and you will have treasure in heaven; then come, follow me.' But his face fell at these words, and he went away sad, for he was a man of great wealth. Mark 10: 17–22

Two mites, two drops (yet all her house and land),
Falls from a steady heart, though trembling hand.
The other's wanton wealth foams high and brave,
The other cast away, she only gave.

Richard Crashaw

A cheerful giver does not count the cost of what he gives. His heart is set on pleasing and cheering him to whom the gift is given. Julian of Norwich

Jesus said to his disciples, 'I tell you solemnly, it will be hard for a rich man to enter the kingdom of heaven.'

Matthew 19: 23

OBEDIENCE

We should rather love obedience than fear disobedience.

St Francis de Sales

You have been obedient to the truth and purified your souls until you can love like brothers in sincerity; let your love for each other be real and from the heart – your new birth was not from any mortal seed but from the everlasting word of the living and everlasting God. What is this word? It is the good news that has been brought to you. 1 Peter 1: 22–25

Almighty, ever-living God,
make us ever obey you willingly and promptly.
Teach us how to serve you
with sincere and upright hearts
in every sphere of life.

The Prayer of the Church

Be strong and show yourself a man. Observe the injunctions of the Lord your God, following his ways and keeping his laws, that so you may be successful in all you do and undertake. 1 Kings 2: 2–3

No man securely commands but he who has
learned to obey.

Thomas à Kempis

I pray that the God of peace, who brought our Lord Jesus back from the dead, may make you ready to do his will in any kind of good action.

Hebrews 13: 20–21

It is not those who say to me, 'Lord, Lord', who will enter the kingdom of heaven, but the person who does the will of my Father in heaven. Matthew 7: 21

Jesus said:
'My food
is to do the will of the one who sent me,
and to complete his work.'

John 4: 34

ANGER

In spite of your anger, Lord, have compassion.

Habbakuk 3: 4

Happy the gentle:
they shall have the earth for their heritage.

Matthew 5: 4

Let your words be for the improvement of others, as occasion offers, and do good to your listeners, otherwise you will only be grieving the Holy Spirit of God who has marked you with his seal for you to be set free when the day comes. Never have grudges against others, or lose your temper, or raise your voice to anybody, or call each other names, or allow any sort of spitefulness. Be friends with one another, and kind, forgiving each other as readily as God forgave you in Christ. Ephesians 4: 29–32

Remember this, my dear brothers: be quick to listen but slow to speak and slow to rouse your temper; God's righteousness is never served by man's anger. Nobody must imagine that he is religious while he still goes on deceiving himself and not keeping control over his tongue; anyone who does this has the wrong idea of religion. James 1: 19–20, 26

I saw full surely that wherever our Lord appears, peace reigns, and anger has no place. For I saw no whit of anger in God. Julian of Norwich

Come back to me with all your heart . . .
Turn to the Lord your God again,
for he is all tenderness and compassion,
slow to anger, rich in graciousness,
and ready to relent.

Joel 2: 12–13

SORROW

God of mercy and compassion,
slow to anger, O Lord,
abounding in love and truth,
turn and take pity on me.

Psalm 85: 15–16

A leper came to Jesus and pleaded on his knees: 'If you want to' he said, 'you can cure me.' Feeling sorry for him Jesus stretched out his hand and touched him. 'Of course I want to!' he said. 'Be cured!' And the leprosy left him at once and he was cured. Mark 1: 14

My God, I am sorry and ask forgiveness for my sins.
By the help of your grace I will try not to sin again.

An Act of Contrition

Naked I came from my mother's womb,
naked I shall return.
The Lord gave, the Lord has taken back.
Blessed be the name of the Lord!

If we take happiness from God's hand, must we not take sorrow too?
Job 1: 21, 2: 10

Jesus Christ, our Saviour, you were like us in all things but sin. Be with me when I am tempted, and stay with me when I fall, so that by your grace I may learn to trust in your strength. Amen.

Lord Jesus Christ, Son of God
have mercy on me, a sinner.
cf. Luke 18: 13

Almighty, ever-living God,
whose love surpasses all that we ask or deserve,
open up for us the treasures of your mercy.
Forgive us all that weighs on our conscience,
and grant us more even than we dare to ask.
We make our prayer through Christ our Lord.
Amen.
A Sunday Prayer

Lord God,
in your goodness have mercy on me:
do not look on my sins,
but take away my guilt.
Create in me a clean heart
and renew within me an upright spirit.

PRAYER

Seek the Lord and he will give life to your soul.

Where two or three meet in my name, I shall be there with them. Matthew 18: 20

To seek God
means first of all
to let yourself be found by him.
He is the God of Abraham, Isaac, and Jacob.
He is the God of Jesus Christ.
He is your God,
not because he is yours, but because you are his.

Rule for a New Brother

When you pray, go to your private room and, when you have shut your door, pray to your Father who is in that secret place, and your Father who sees all that is done in secret will reward you. Matthew 6: 6

Like the deer that yearns
for running streams,
so my soul is yearning
for you my God.

Psalm 41 (42): 1

You should be awake, and praying not to be put to the test. The spirit is willing, but the flesh is weak.

Mark 14: 38

Ask, and it will be given to you; search, and you will find; knock, and the door will be opened to you. For the one who asks always receives; the one who searches always finds; the one who knocks will always have the door opened to him. . . . If you who are evil, know how to give your children what is good, how much more will your Father in heaven give good things to those who ask him! Matthew 7: 7–11

My eyes watch for you before dawn.
from Psalm 118 (119): 148

Ask and you will receive, and so your joy will be complete.

John 16: 24

We fly to thy patronage,
O holy Mother of God;
Despise not our petitions in our necessities,
but deliver us always from all dangers,
O glorious and blessed virgin.

Traditional

I called with all my heart; Lord, hear me.

ANXIETY

Lord, listen to my cry,
for I am in the depths of distress.
Psalm 141 (142): 7

Does a woman forget her baby at the breast,
or fail to cherish the son of her womb?
Yet even if these forget,
I will never forget you, says the Lord God.
Isaiah 49: 15

Jesus said, 'Come to me, all you who labour and are overburdened, and I will give you rest. Shoulder my yoke and learn from me, for I am gentle and humble in heart, and you will find rest for your souls. Yes, my yoke is easy and my burden light.' Matthew 11: 28–30

Jesus said to his disciples: 'This is why I am telling you not to worry about your life and what you are to eat, nor about your body and how you are to clothe it. For life means more than food, and the body more than clothing. There is no need to be afraid, little flock, for it has pleased your Father to give you the kingdom.'
Luke 12: 22–3, 32

Blessed be the God and Father of our Lord Jesus Christ, a gentle Father and the God of all consolation, who comforts us in all our sorrows, so that we can offer others, in their sorrows, the consolation that we have received from God ourselves. Indeed, as the sufferings of Christ overflow to us, so, through Christ, does our consolation overflow. 2 Corinthians 1: 3–5

I called to the Lord in my distress;
he answered and freed me.
The Lord is at my side, I do not fear.
Psalm 117 (118): 5–6

Deliver us, Lord, from every evil,
and grant us peace in our day.
In your mercy keep us free from sin
and protect us from all anxiety
as we wait in joyful hope
for the coming of our Saviour, Jesus Christ. Amen.
A Prayer before Communion

Christ has said, 'My grace is enough for you, my power is at its best in weakness'. So I shall be very happy to make my weaknesses my special boast so that the power of Christ may stay over me, and that is why I am quite content with my weaknesses, and with insults, hardships, persecution, and the agonies I go through for Christ's sake. For it is when I am weak that I am strong. 2 Corinthians 12: 9–10

FAMILY

Guard your family, Lord, with constant loving
care
for in your divine grace we place our only hope.
The Prayer of the Church

Lord, bless the household of which I form a part. Show us how we can help one another, share our interests and sorrows and joys with one another, be ready to make sacrifices for one another. I ask that I may find my joy in serving them as you found your joy in serving Mary and Joseph on earth. Hubert van Zeller

Jesus exclaimed, 'I bless you, Father, Lord of heaven and of earth, for hiding these things from the learned and the clever, and revealing them to mere children.'
Matthew 11: 25

Jesus said, 'I tell you solemnly, unless you change and become like little children you will never enter the kingdom of heaven. And so, the one who makes himself as little as this little child will be the greatest in the kingdom of heaven.' Matthew 18: 3–4

Anyone who welcomes one of these little children in my name, welcomes me; and anyone who welcomes me welcomes not me but the one who sent me.

Mark 9: 37

A wife should regard her husband as she regards Jesus Christ. Just as Christ is head of the Church and saves her, so is a husband the head of the family. A husband must love his wife just as Christ loved the Church and gave himself for her. Children have a duty to obey their parents. The commandment, 'Love your parents,' carries with it this promise, 'You will do well and live happily.' On their part, parents must never make their children resentful, but should bring them up, correct them, and guide them as the Lord does. Finally, grow strong in the Lord, with his strength. Pray all the time for whatever you need, under the guidance of the Holy Spirit. *from* Ephesians 5 and 6

As long as we love one another
God will live in us,
and his love will be complete in us.

1 John 4: 12

Out of his infinite glory, may the Father give you the power through his Spirit for your hidden self to grow strong, so that Christ may live in your hearts through faith, and then, planted in love and built on love, you will with all the saints have strength to grasp the breadth and the length, the height and the depth; until, knowing the love of Christ, which is beyond all knowledge, you are filled with the utter fulness of God.

Ephesians 3: 16–19

THE DAY'S WORK

When I see the heavens, the work of your hands,
the moon and the stars which you arranged
what is man that you should keep him in mind,
mortal man that you care for him?
Yet you have made him little less than a god;
with glory and honour you crowned him,
gave him power over the works of your hand,
put all things under his feet.

Psalm 8: 4–7

Don't delude yourself into thinking that God can be cheated: where a man sows, there he reaps: if he sows in the field of self-indulgence he will get a harvest of corruption out of it; if he sows in the field of the Spirit he will get from it a harvest of eternal life. We must never get tired of doing good because if we don't give up the struggle we shall get our harvest at the proper time. While we have the chance, we must do good to all, and especially to our brothers in the faith.

Galatians 6: 7–10

We beg you to pay proper respect to those who work with you, those whom the Lord has chosen to guide and instruct you. Treat them with the greatest respect and love, because of the work they do. Be at peace among yourselves.

1 Thessalonians 5: 12–13

Lord, be the beginning and end
of all that we do and say.
Prompt our actions with your grace
and complete them with your all-powerful help.
Through Christ our Lord. Amen.

A Sunday Prayer

Father, I dedicate this new day to you;
as I go about my work, I ask you to bless those I come into contact with.
Lord, I pray for all men and women who work to earn their living;
give them satisfaction in what they do.
Spirit of God, comfort the unemployed and their families;
they are your children and my brothers and sisters.
I ask you to help them find work soon.

Teach us, good Lord, to serve you as you deserve;
to give and not to count the cost;
to fight and not to heed the wounds;
to toil and not to seek for rest;
to labour and to ask for no reward,
save that of knowing that we do your will;
through Christ our Lord.

St Ignatius

God, Lord and Master of the vineyard,
you allot us our task,
and determine the just rewards of our labours.
Help us to bear the burden of the day
and accept your will in all things without complaint.
Through Christ our Lord. Amen.

The Prayer of the Church

Blessed are you, Lord God of all creation,
through your goodness we enjoy those things
that are the fruits of the earth and the work of our hands,
may they be for us a source of lasting life.
Blessed be God for ever.

Jesus Christ, the Truth

In the beginning was the Word
the Word was with God
and the Word was God.

John 1: 1

Truth is eternal and unchanging. 'Your truth, O Lord, will last from age to age.' Jesus promised to send his Spirit to lead us to all truth. This truth is the ground of our faith, the source of self-knowledge, the beginning of forgiveness and healing, the basis of justice and of peace; it is the cause of our joy; it is expressed in law; it is the only true foundation of unity.

SPIRIT

I shall ask the Father,
and he will give you another Advocate
to be with you for ever,
the Spirit of Truth.
The Advocate, the Holy Spirit,
whom the Father will send in my name,
will teach you everything
and remind you of all I have said to you.

John 14: 16–17, 26

Your body, you know, is the temple of the Holy Spirit, who is in you since you received him from God. That is why you should use your body for the glory of God.
1 Corinthians 6: 19–20

I shall give you a new heart, and put a new spirit in you; I shall remove the heart of stone from your bodies and give you a heart of flesh instead. I shall put my Spirit in you, and make you keep my laws and sincerely respect my observances. You shall be my people and I will be your God.
Ezekiel 36: 25–7

In the one Spirit we were all baptised.
1 Corinthians 12: 13

Everyone moved by the Spirit is a son of God. The Spirit you received is not the spirit of slaves bringing fear into your lives again; it is the spirit of sons, and it makes us cry out, 'Abba, Father!'. The Spirit himself and our spirit bear united witness that we are children of God.

The Spirit too comes to help us in our weakness. For when we cannot choose words in order to pray properly, the Spirit himself expresses our plea in a way that could never be put into words, and God who knows everything in our hearts knows perfectly well what he means, and that the pleas of the saints expressed by the Spirit are according to the mind of God.

Romans 8: 14–16, 26–7

Holy Spirit of God, sent by the Father and the Son, fill my heart with your love. Lead me to know myself, to root out my selfishness, and to share with others the fruits of your presence: love, joy, peace, patience, kindness, goodness, trustfulness, gentleness and self-control. cf. Galatians 5: 22

FAITH

In God alone is my soul at rest;
my help comes from him.
He alone is my rock, my stronghold,
my fortress: I stand firm.

Psalm 61 (62): 2–3

Jesus said: 'I tell you solemnly, if your faith were the size of a mustard seed you could say to this mountain, "Move from here to there," and it would move; nothing would be impossible for you.' Matthew 17: 20–1

Jesus said:
'I am the resurrection.
If anyone believes in me, even though he dies he will live
and whoever lives and believes in me
will never die.'

John 11: 25–26

Jesus said: 'Doubt no longer but believe.' Thomas replied, 'My Lord and my God.' Jesus said to him, 'You believe because you can see me. Happy are those who have not seen and yet believe.' John 20: 27–9

Jesus said: 'If anyone declares himself for me in the presence of men, I will declare myself for him in the presence of my Father in heaven. But the one who disowns me in the presence of men, I will disown him in the presence of my Father in heaven.'
Matthew 10: 32–3

Lord I believe! Help what little faith I have.
Mark 9: 25

By whatever means he teaches us, his will is that we perceive him wisely, receive him joyfully, and keep ourselves in him faithfully. Julian of Norwich

Be calm but vigilant, because your enemy the devil is prowling round like a roaring lion, looking for someone to eat. Stand up to him, strong in faith and in the knowledge that your brothers all over the world are suffering the same things. You will have to suffer only for a little while. The God of all grace will see that all is well again; he will confirm, strengthen and support you. His power lasts for ever and ever. Amen.
1 Peter 5: 8–11

Your word is a lamp for my steps
and a light for my path.
Psalm 118 (119): 105

We have never failed to remember you in our prayers and to give thanks for you to God, the Father of our Lord Jesus Christ, ever since we heard about your faith in Christ Jesus and the love that you show towards all the saints because of the hope which is stored up for you in heaven. Colossians 1: 3–4

O my God, I believe in you, and all that your Church teaches, because you have said it, and your word is true.
An Act of Faith

Lord God,
since by the adoption of grace
you have made us children of light:
do not let false doctrine darken our minds,
but grant that your light may shine within us
and we may always live in the brightness of truth.
A Sunday Prayer

It is by grace that you have been saved, through faith; not by anything of your own, but by a gift from God. We are God's work of art, created in Christ Jesus to live the good life as from the beginning he had meant us to live it.
Ephesians 2: 8–10

I believe in God, the Father Almighty,
creator of heaven and earth;
and in Jesus Christ, his only Son, our Lord;
who was conceived by the Holy Spirit,
born of the Virgin Mary,
suffered under Pontius Pilate,
was crucified, died and was buried.
He descended into hell;
the third day he rose again from the dead.
He ascended into heaven
and sits at the right hand of God the almighty
Father.
From thence he will come to judge the living and
the dead.
I believe in the Holy Spirit;
the holy catholic Church;
the communion of saints;
the forgiveness of sins;
the resurrection of the body;
and the life everlasting. Amen.
The Apostles' Creed

HUMILITY

Wrap yourselves in humility to be servants of each other, because God refuses the proud and will always favour the humble. Bow down, then, before the power of God now, and he will raise you up on the appointed day. 1 Peter 5: 5–6

In your minds you must be the same as Christ Jesus:
His state was divine,
yet he did not cling
to his equality with God
but emptied himself
to assume the condition of a slave,
and became as men are;
and being as all men are,
he was humbler yet,
even to accepting death,
death on a cross.
But God raised him high
and gave him the name
which is above all other names
so that all beings
in the heavens, on earth and in the underworld,
should bend the knee at the name of Jesus
and that every tongue should acclaim
Jesus Christ as Lord,
to the glory of God the Father.

Philippians 2: 6–11

The Lord guides the humble in the right path.

Unless you become like little children you will not enter into the kingdom of heaven. Matthew 18: 3

Learn from me, for I am gentle and humble in heart.
Matthew 11: 29

God does not see as man sees; man looks at appearances but the Lord looks at the heart. 1 Samuel 16: 7

My soul glorifies the Lord,
my spirit rejoices in God, my saviour.
He looks on his servant in her lowliness;
henceforth all ages will call me blessed.

The Almighty works marvels for me.
Holy his name!
His mercy is from age to age,
on those who fear him.

He puts forth his arm in strength
and scatters the proud-hearted.
He casts the mighty from their thrones
and raises the lowly.

He fills the starving with good things,
and sends the rich away empty.

He protects Israel, his servant,
remembering his mercy,
the mercy promised to our fathers,
to Abraham and his sons for ever.

The Magnificat

The first degree of humility is obedience without delay.

St Benedict

In all my walks it seems to me
that the grace of God lies in courtesy.

Hilaire Belloc

Almighty God, take from me all vainglorious thoughts, all desires for mine own praise, all envy, covetousness, gluttony, sloth and lechery, all wrathful affections, all desire for revenge, all delight in harm to others, all pleasure in provoking them to wrath and anger, all delight in upbraiding and insulting them in their affliction and calamity. Give freely unto me, good Lord, thy love and favour which my love for thee, be it ever so great, could not receive except out of thine own great goodness.

St Thomas More

FORGIVENESS

Forgive us our trespasses,
as we forgive those who trespass against us.
The *Our Father*

Jesus said: 'If you forgive others their failings, your heavenly Father will forgive you yours, but if you do not forgive others, your Father will not forgive your failings either.' Matthew 6: 14–15

Then Peter came up to Jesus and said: 'Lord, how often must I forgive my brother if he wrongs me? As often as seven times?' Jesus answered, 'Not seven, I tell you, but seventy-seven times'. Matthew 18: 21–22

Jesus said: 'Be compassionate as your Father is compassionate.' Luke 6: 36

You are God's chosen race, his saints; he loves you, and you should be clothed in sincere compassion, in kindness and humility, gentleness and patience. Bear with one another; forgive each other as soon as a quarrel begins. The Lord has forgiven you; now you must do the same. Over all these clothes, to keep them together and complete them, put on love. And may the peace of Christ reign in your hearts, because it was for this that you were called together as parts of one body. Always be thankful. Colossians 3: 12–15

Father, forgive them; they do not know what they are doing. Luke 23: 34

Give me thy grace, good Lord:
to set the world at nought,
to set my mind fast upon thee,
and not to hang upon the blast of men's mouths.
To be content to be solitary.
Not to long for worldly company.
Little and little utterly to cast off the world,
and rid my mind of all the business thereof.
Not to long to hear of any worldly things.
But that the hearing of worldly phantasies
may be to me displeasant.
Gladly to be thinking of God.
Piteously to call for his help.
To lean upon the comfort of God.
Busily to labour to love him.
To know mine own violence and wretchedness.
To humble myself under the mighty hand of God.
To bewail my sins passed.
For the purging of them patiently to suffer
adversity.
Gladly to bear my purgatory here.
To be joyful of tribulations.

St Thomas More

Heal my soul for I have sinned against you.

Grant me, O God, so worthily to receive this most holy body and blood of thy Son that I may thereby receive the forgiveness of all my sins, be filled with thy Holy Spirit, and find peace. For thou only art God and there is no other besides thee. *The Sarum Missal*

To those who love you, Lord,
you promise to come with your Son
and make your home within them.
Come then with your purifying grace
and make our hearts a place where you can dwell.
A Sunday Prayer

Look in love on all whose sins have separated
them from you.
Reconcile them to yourself and to your Church.
Bidding Prayer

Cry wrenched wrung wounded radiant hearts
'O Christ, forgive!'
Beg nailed gnarled bloodied Christened hands,
'Dear Jesu, bless!'
Smile blind burnt sunken glowing eyes,
'Have mercy, Lord!'
Plead toiled torn aching tempered frames,
'Sweet Master, save!'

Holy Father,
you know both our strength and our weakness.
Help us to know ourselves better
so that we will always judge ourselves
honestly and openly.
May we be guided by your Holy Spirit
who with you and your Son
is the source of all love and knowledge.
Never grow tired of what is right.
2 Thessalonians 3: 13

Enlighten our minds, O God, and purify our desires. Correct our wanderings and pardon our defects, so that by thy guidance we may be preserved from making shipwreck of our faith, be kept in a good conscience, and at length be landed in the safe haven of eternal peace. Through Jesus Christ our Lord. Amen.

St Anselm

HEALING

The Son of Man has come to seek out and save
what was lost.

Luke 19: 10

Come to me all you who labour and are overburdened, and I will give you rest. Shoulder my yoke and learn from me, for I am gentle and humble in heart, and you will find rest for your souls. Yes, my yoke is easy and my burden light. Matthew 11: 28–30

I tell you that her sins, her many sins, must have been forgiven her, or she would not have shown such great love. It is the man who is forgiven little who shows little love . . . Your faith has saved you; go in peace.

Luke 7: 47–50

Help us, O Lord our God, since we cannot flee from the body, or the body flee from us. We must needs carry about the body, because it is bound up with us. We cannot destroy it; we are forced to preserve it. But the world surrounds us and assails us through the five gateways of sense. St Bernard

O Lord, I cried to you for help and you have
healed me.
I will thank you for ever.

Psalm 29 (30): 3, 13

Lord, support us as we pray,
protect us day and night,
so that we who under your guiding hand
live in a world of change,
may always draw strength from you,
with whom there is no shadow of alteration.

Evening Prayer

I lift up my eyes to the mountains;
from where shall come my help?
My help shall come from the Lord
who made heaven and earth.

Psalm 120 (121): 1–2

JUSTICE

Justice and right are the pillars of your throne, O Lord, love and truth walk in your presence.

Psalm 88 (89): 15

Jesus said to the rich young man: 'There is still one thing you lack. Sell all that you own and distribute the money to the poor, and you will have treasure in heaven; then come, follow me.' Luke 18: 22

'Blessed are those who hunger and thirst for justice; they shall have their fill.' Matthew 5: 6

Almighty Father, bring justice to our world, that your people may live in the joy of your peace.

Bidding Prayer

This is what the Lord asks of you:
only this, to act justly,
to love tenderly,
and to walk humbly with your God.

Micah 6: 8

If a man who was rich enough in this world's goods
saw that one of his brothers was in need,
but closed his heart to him,
how could the love of God live in him?
My children,
our love is not to be just words or mere talk,
but something real and active.

1 John 3: 17–18

Do not be afraid of any man, for the judgement is God's.

Deuteronomy 1: 17

Lord, make me an instrument of your peace:
Where there is hatred, let me sow love;
where there is injury, let me sow pardon;
where there is doubt, let me sow faith;
where there is despair, let me give hope;
where there is darkness, let me give light;
where there is sadness, let me give joy.

O Divine Master, grant that I may try
not to be comforted, but to comfort;
not to be understood, but to understand;
not to be loved, but to love.
Because it is in giving that we receive,
it is in forgiving that we are forgiven,
and it is in dying that we are born to eternal life.

St Francis of Assisi

True Light of the World, Lord Jesus Christ,
as you enlighten all men for their salvation,
give us grace, we pray,
to herald your coming
by preparing the ways of justice and of peace.

Morning Prayer

PEACE

Truly I have set my soul in silence and peace.
A weaned child on its mother's breast even so is my soul. Psalm 130 (131): 2

May the Lord of peace himself give you peace all the time and in every way. 2 Thessalonians 3: 16

He was pierced through for our faults, crushed for our sins.
On him lies a punishment that brings us peace,
and through his wounds we are healed.
Isaiah 53: 6

Be at peace, and know that nothing can separate you from the love of God made visible in Christ Jesus our Lord. Romans 8: 39

Jesus came and stood among them. 'Peace be with you' he said to them. The disciples were filled with joy when they saw the Lord, and he said to them again, 'Peace be with you'. John 20: 20–21

Lord Jesus Christ, you said to your apostles:
'I leave you peace, my peace I give you'.
Look not on our sins, but on the faith of your Church,
and grant us the peace and unity of your kingdom where you live for ever and ever. Amen.
A Prayer before Communion

Guide our steps, good Lord, in the ways of your service, and forgive us our sins, that we may discover the gift of your peace and share it with others.
The Prayer of the Church

Blessed are the peacemakers, they shall be called the sons of God. Matthew 6: 9

Deep peace of the running wave to you.
Deep peace of the flowing air to you.
Deep peace of the quiet earth to you.
Deep peace of the shining stars to you.
Deep peace of the Son of Peace to you.

Irish Blessing

There is no need to worry; but if there is anything you need, pray for it, asking God for it with prayer and thanksgiving, and that peace of God, which is so much greater than we can understand, will guard your hearts and your thoughts, in Christ Jesus. Then the God of peace will be with you. Philippians 4: 6–9

The soul is immediately at one with God, when it is truly at peace in itself. Julian of Norwich

Give us perfect peace, Lord,
so that we may delight in serving you,
all the days of our life,
and at the last, with our Lady's help,
come safely to your presence.

Midday Prayer

Lord, give peace to our troubled world; and give to your children security of mind and freedom from anxiety.

Bidding Prayer

JOY

Like the deer that yearns
for running streams,
so my soul is yearning
for you, my God.

Psalm 41 (42): 2

Jesus said:
'You are sad now, but I shall see you again,
and your hearts will be full of joy,
and that joy no one shall take from you.'

John 16: 22

Be happy at all times; pray constantly; and for all things give thanks to God, because this is what God expects you to do in Christ Jesus.

1 Thessalonians 13: 16–18

Fixing his eyes on his disciples Jesus said:
'How happy are you who are poor,
yours is the kingdom of God.
Happy you who are hungry now, you shall be satisfied.
Happy you who weep now, you shall laugh.'

Luke 6: 20–1

Rejoice in the Lord always, and again I say rejoice.

Philippians 4: 4

My heart rejoices, my soul is glad;
even my body shall rest in safety.
You will show me the path of life,
the fulness of joy in your presence,
at your right hand happiness for ever.

Psalm 15 (16): 9–11

If you abide in love
you will abide in God
and not wander any more in darkness.

Then live in joyfulness and hope
unanxious, without any trace of fear,
at peace with yourself and the world,
in ceaseless reverence and thanks.
Because God's love for you endures for ever.

Rule for a New Brother

Lord God,
you are the source of all that is good,
of all that brings joy.
Help us to rejoice always in you
and to share our joy with others.

He will never have full joy in us until we have full joy in him, truly seeing his lovely blessed face.

Julian of Norwich

LAW

'Heaven and earth will pass away but my words will not pass away, says the Lord. Matthew 24: 35

Let your love come and I shall live,
for your law is my delight.

Psalm 118 (119): 77

May your hearts be wholly with the Lord our God,
following his laws and keeping his commandments.

1 Kings 8: 61

A wise man will not hate the law,
but he who is hypocritical about it
is like a boat in a storm.

Ecclesiasticus 33: 2

Avoid getting into debt, except the debt of mutual love. If you love your fellow men you have carried out your obligation. All the commandments are summed up in this single command: you must love your neighbour as yourself. Love is the one thing that cannot hurt your neighbour: that is why it is the answer to every one of the commandments. Romans 13: 8–11

Help us to keep your commandments, so that through your Holy Spirit we may dwell in you, and you in us.
Bidding Prayer

Shed your clear light on our hearts, Lord,
that walking continually in the way of your
  commandments,
we may never be deceived or misled.
Morning Prayer

This is the covenant I will make with you – it is the Lord who speaks. Deep within you I will plant my Law, writing it on your hearts. Then I will be your God and you shall be my people. *from* Jeremiah 31: 33

Love and do what you will.
St Augustine

When you have done all you have been told to do, say, 'We are merely servants: we have done no more than our duty'. Luke 17: 10

UNITY

In the meantime brothers we wish you happiness; try to be perfect; help one another. Be united; live in peace, and the God of love and peace will be with you. The grace of our Lord Jesus Christ, the love of God and the fellowship of the Holy Spirit be with you all.
2 Corinthians 13: 11–13

May the peace of Christ reign in your hearts, because it is for this that you are called together as parts of one body. Colossians 3: 15

May he who helps us when we refuse to give up, help you all to be tolerant with each other, following the example of Christ Jesus, so that united in mind and voice you may give glory to the God and Father of our Lord Jesus Christ. Romans 15: 5–6

I implore you therefore to lead a life worthy of your vocation. Bear with one another charitably, in complete selflessness, gentleness and patience. Do all you can to preserve the unity of the Spirit by the peace that binds you together. There is one Body, one Spirit, just as you were all called into one and the same hope when you were called. There is one Lord, one Faith, one baptism, and one God who is Father of all, over all, through all, and within all. Ephesians 4: 1–6

Each one of us, however, has been given his own share of grace, given as Christ allotted it. And to some, his gift was that they should be apostles; to some, prophets; to some, evangelists; to some, pastors and teachers; so that the saints together make a unity in the work of service, building up the Body of Christ. In this way we are all to come to unity in our faith and our knowledge of the Son of God, until we become perfect Man, fully mature with the fulness of Christ himself. Ephesians 4: 9–13

Let us pray that all men,
of every race and nation,
may acknowledge the one God as Father,
and in the bond of common brotherhood
seek his kingdom,
which is peace and joy in the Holy Spirit.
Bidding Prayer, Confirmation

Jesus Christ, the Life

God created man in the image of himself,
in the image of God he created them,
male and female he created them.

Genesis 1: 27

Jesus said:

'I have come so that they may have life,
and have it to the full.'

John 10: 10

Jesus died so that we could share God's life. To find this fulness of life we must die to self, be converted, be patient in our sufferings and uncertainties, be willing to grow in hope and love. As we become more aware of God's presence in our lives, and of the world he has made, so we are ready to adore, to praise and to thank him. By sharing the life of Christ in his Church we discover something of the freedom of the sons and daughters of God.

DEATH

Remember our brothers and sisters
who have gone to their rest
in the hope of rising again;
bring them and all the departed
into the light of your presence.

Eucharistic Prayer

Death was never of God's fashioning; not for his pleasure does life cease to be; what meant his creation, but that all created things should have being? No breed has he created on earth but for its thriving; none carries in itself the seeds of its own destruction. Think not that mortality bears sway on earth; no end or term is fixed to a life well lived. Wisdom 1: 13–15

My soul is thirsting for God,
the God of my life;
when can I enter and see
the face of God?

Psalm 41 (42): 3

We pray for those who have died, and are on their way to you, Lord.
Give them fulness of life and happiness.

We pray for those who are dying, Lord, and who are afraid.
Give them strength to go on their last journey in peace.

We pray, Lord, for those who have been wounded by the death of one they love.
Help them find the new life that comes through death.

We pray for those who are worried and anxious about many things.
Help them, Lord, find peace in dying to themselves.

We pray for those who are depressed and in despair.
Show them, Lord, that by dying to self there is a birth of hope.

Bidding Prayers

Lord, Lord, do you hear me?
Lord, show me my door,
take me by the hand.
Open the door,
show me the way,
the path leading to joy, to light.

Michel Quoist

Christ is the morning star
who when the darkness of this world is past
brings to his saints the promise of the light of life
and opens everlasting day.

St Bede

Let the absolving words be said over me, and the holy oil sign and seal me, and thy own body be my food and thy blood my sprinkling. And let my mother Mary breathe on me and my angel whisper peace to me, and my saints smile on me . . . that in them all and through them all I may receive the gift of perseverance, and die, as I desire to live, in thy faith, in thy Church, in thy service, and in thy love. Cardinal Newman

Lord God,
you have prepared for those who love you
what no eye has seen, no ear has heard.
Fill our hearts with your love,
so that loving you above all and in all,
we may attain your promises
which the heart of man has not conceived.
Sunday Prayer

If we have died with him, then we shall live with him.
If we hold firm, then we shall reign with him.
If we disown him, then he will disown us.
We may be unfaithful, but he is always faithful,
for he cannot disown his own self.
2 Timothy 2: 11–13

Day is done, but love unfailing
dwells ever here;
shadows fall, but hope prevailing
calms every fear.
Loving Father, none forsaking,
take our hearts, of love's own making,
watch our sleeping, guard our waking,
be always near!

Dark descends, but light unending
shines through our night;
you are with us, ever lending
new strength to sight;
one in love, your truth confessing,
one in hope of heaven's blessing,
may we see, in love's possessing,
love's endless light! James Quinn

The throne of God and of the Lamb will be in its place in the city; his servants will worship him, they will see him face to face, and his name will be written on their foreheads. It will never be night again and they will not need lamplight or sunlight, because the Lord God will be shining on them. They will reign for ever and ever. Revelation 22: 3–5

Father, into your hands I commit my spirit.
Luke 23: 46

I am the resurrection.
If anyone believes in me, even though he dies, he will live,
and whoever lives and believes in me
will never die.
John 11: 25–26

I tell you, most solemnly,
unless a wheat grain falls on the ground and dies,
it remains only a single grain;
but if it dies,
it yields a rich harvest.
Anyone who loves his life loses it;
anyone who hates his life in this world
will keep it for the eternal life.
John 12: 24–25

I tell you most solemnly,
whoever keeps my word
will never see death.
John 8: 51

Anyone who finds his life will lose it; anyone who loses his life for my sake will find it. Matthew 10: 39

Come, Lord Jesus, come!
Revelation 22: 20

CONVERSION

Repent and be converted, for the kingdom of God is at hand.
Matthew 3: 8

Give me, good Lord, a full faith and a fervent charity, a love of you, good Lord, incomparable above the love of myself; and that I love nothing to your displeasure but everything in an order to you.

Take from me, good Lord, this lukewarm fashion, or rather key-cold manner of meditation and this dullness in praying to you. And give me warmth, delight and life in thinking about you. And give me your grace to long for your holy Sacraments and specially to rejoice in the presence of your blessed Body, sweet Saviour Christ, in the holy Sacrament of the Altar, and duly to thank you for your gracious coming.

St Thomas More

The Son of Man has come to seek out and save what was lost.
Luke 19: 10

As by your will you first strayed away from God, so now turn back and search for him ten times as hard.
Baruch 4: 28–29

Soul of Christ, sanctify me.
Body of Christ, save me.
Water from the side of Christ, wash me.
Passion of Christ, strengthen me.
O Good Jesu, hear me.
Let me not be separated from you.
From the malicious enemy defend me.
In the hour of my death call me.
And bid me come to you,
so that with your saints I may praise you,
for ever and ever. Amen.

I will make an everlasting covenant with them; I will not cease in my efforts for their good, and I will put respect for me into their hearts, so that they turn from me no more. Jeremiah 32: 40

I tell you solemnly, unless you change and become as little children, you will never enter the kingdom of heaven. Matthew 18: 3

Your mind must be renewed by a spiritual revolution, so that you can put on the new self that has been created in God's way, in the goodness and holiness of the truth. Ephesians 4: 24

O God, give me the sincerity
to accept the things I cannot change,
the courage to change the things I can,
and the wisdom to know the difference.
Rheinhold Niebuhr

PATIENCE

Suffering brings patience, as we know, and patience brings perseverance, and perseverance brings hope, and this hope is not deceptive, because the love of God has been poured into our hearts by the Holy Spirit which has been given us. Romans 5: 4–5

With the Lord 'a day' can mean a thousand years. The Lord is not being slow to carry out his promises, as anybody else might be called slow, but he is being patient with you all, wanting nobody to be lost and everybody to be brought to change his ways.

2 Peter 3: 8–9

Love is always patient and kind.

1 Corinthians 13: 4

Remember, O most loving Virgin Mary, that it is a thing unheard of, that anyone ever had recourse to your protection, implored your help, or sought your intercession, and was left forsaken. Filled therefore with confidence in your goodness I fly to you, O Mother, Virgin of virgins. To you I come, before you I stand, a sorrowful sinner. Despise not my poor words, O Mother of the Word of God, but graciously hear and grant my prayer. St Bernard

Lord, give me patience in tribulation. Let the memory of your Passion, and of those bitter pains you suffered for me, strengthen my patience and support me in this tribulation and adversity. St John Forrest

Give patient tolerance, Lord, to all who are no longer young. Open the hearts of the young to accept from them understanding and love. Bidding Prayer

Never disappoint the trust
another man puts in you.
Be warm and merciful
and let none go from you empty-handed.
The least you can offer
is your time and patience,
your affection and your prayer.

Rule for a New Brother

O Lord my God, as you led your people through the desert, so lead me now through the desert of my failures to your kingdom. Light my way; show me your will; give me your Spirit of truth, so that I may know, love and serve you more faithfully.

SUFFERING

All shall be well, and all shall be well, and all manner of things shall be well. Julian of Norwich

Lord, in answer to our prayer
give us patience in suffering hardships
after the example of your Only-begotten Son,
who lives and reigns for ever and ever. Amen.

Midday Prayer

Lord, teach us to see you present in all men. Help us to recognise you most of all in those who suffer.

Bidding Prayer

My Father, if it is possible, let this cup pass me by. Nevertheless, let it be as you, not I, would have it. My Father, if this cup cannot pass by without my drinking it, your will be done! Matthew 26: 39, 42

The spirit is willing, but the flesh is weak.

Matthew 26: 41

I think that what we suffer in this life can never be compared to the glory, as yet unrevealed, which is waiting for us. The whole creation is eagerly waiting for God to reveal his sons . . . And not only creation, but all of us who possess the first fruits of the Spirit, we too groan inwardly as we wait for our bodies to be set free . . . We must wait with patience.

from Romans 8: 18–25

I have been crucified with Christ, and I live now not with my own life but with the life of Christ who lives in me.

Galatians 2: 19–20

> My God, my God, why have you forsaken me?
> Do not leave me alone in my distress;
> Come close, there is none else to help.
>
> O Lord, do not leave me alone,
> my strength, make haste to help me!

Psalm 21 (22): 2, 12, 20

Lord, be with those who are persecuted for their faith, and those cut off from the support of the Church; good Shepherd, in their pain and desolation may they know your tender care.

Bidding Prayer

GROWTH

What we ask God is that through perfect wisdom and spiritual understanding you should reach the fullest knowledge of his will. So you will be able to lead the kind of life the Lord expects of you, a life acceptable to him in all its aspects; showing the results in all the good actions you do and increasing your knowledge of God. You will have in you the strength, based on his own glorious power, never to give in, but to bear anything joyfully, thanking the Father who has made it possible for you to join the saints and with them to inherit the light. Colossians 1: 9–12

Do not let your love be a pretence, but sincerely prefer good to evil. Love each other as much as brothers should, and have a profound respect for each other. Work for the Lord with untiring effort and with great earnestness of spirit. If you have hope, this will make you cheerful. Do not give up if trials come; and keep on praying. Romans 12: 9–12

You will always have your trials but, when they come, try to treat them as a happy privilege; you understand that your faith is only put to the test to make you patient, but patience too is to have its practical result so that you will become fully developed, complete, with nothing missing. James 1: 2–4

The glory of God is man made fully alive.
Saint Irenaeus

How high thou art in the height, how deep in the depth. Thou never leavest us, yet how hard it is to return to thee. Come, Lord, and work. Arouse and incite us. Kindle us and sweep us onward. Be fragrant as flowers, sweet as honey. Teach us to love and to run.
St Augustine

Jesus said:
'I tell you most solemnly
if you do not eat the flesh of the Son of Man
and drink his blood
you will not have life in you.
Anyone who does eat my flesh and drink my blood
has eternal life,
and I shall raise him up on the last day.
For my flesh is real food
and my blood is real drink.
He who eats my flesh and drinks my blood
lives in me
and I live in him . . .
Anyone who eats this bread will live for ever.'

John 6: 53–58

Almighty God and Father, you so loved the world that you sent your Son to show us how to love without limit. Teach me to accept your Spirit of love and truth so that I may learn to live as your friend.

Personal growth is not optional for us . . . God's will that we must grow sums up our human duty.

Pope Paul VI

HOPE

The Lord is my shepherd;
there is nothing I shall want.
Fresh and green are the pastures
where he gives me repose.
Near restful waters he leads me,
to revive my drooping spirit.

Psalm 22 (23): 1–3

Let us be confident in approaching the throne of grace, that we shall have mercy from him and find grace when we are in need of help. Hebrews 4: 16

When I fear, I will trust in you
in God whose word I praise.
In God I trust, I shall not fear:
what can mortal man do to me?

Psalm 55 (56): 4–5

Jesus said: 'Today you will be with me in paradise.'

Luke 23: 24

We are in difficulties on all sides, but never cornered; we see no answer to our problems, but never despair; we have been persecuted, but never deserted; knocked down, but never killed; always, wherever we may be we carry with us in our body the death of Jesus, so that the life of Jesus, too, may always be seen in our body.

2 Corinthians 4: 8–10

O God, to whom all hearts are open, all desires known, and from whom no secrets are hidden, cleanse the thoughts of our hearts by the inpouring of your Holy Spirit, that every thought and word of ours may begin from you, and in you be perfectly completed, through Christ our Lord. Amen.

Redeem me Lord, and show me your mercy.

Psalm 25 (26): 11

A blessing on the man who puts his trust in the
Lord, with the Lord for his hope.
He is like a tree by the waterside,
that thrusts its roots to the stream:
when the heat comes it feels no alarm,
its foliage stays green;
it has no worries in a year of drought,
and never ceases to bear fruit.

Jeremiah 17: 7–8

Lord, happy the man who trusts in you!

Psalm 33 (34): 9

O God, the creator and redeemer of all the faithful, grant to the souls of your servants departed the remission of all their sins, that through our prayers they may obtain that pardon which they have always desired.

LOVE

Lord God,
you love us as a father loves his children.
Help us to respond to your gift
and learn to love without limit,
as did your Son,
Jesus Christ, our Lord.

Love is always patient and kind; it is never jealous; love is never boastful or conceited; it is never rude or selfish; it does not take offence, and is not resentful. Love takes no pleasure in other people's sins but delights in the truth; it is always ready to excuse, to trust, to hope, and to endure whatever comes . . . There are three things that last: faith, hope and love; and the greatest of these is love. 1 Corinthians 13: 4–13

God of your goodness give me yourself, for you are enough for me. Julian of Norwich

May the Lord be generous in increasing your love and make you love one another and the whole human race . . . and may he so confirm your hearts in holiness that you may be blameless in the sight of our God and Father when our Lord Jesus Christ comes with all his saints. 1 Thessalonians 3: 12, 13

God is love
and anyone who lives in love lives in God,
and God lives in him. 1 John 4: 16

The perfect lover longeth for to be
In presence of his love both night and day
And if it haply so befall that he may not be as he would,
He will yet as he may ever be with his love.

St Thomas More

Jesus, Jesus, Jesus
Jesus, Jesus, Jesus
Jesus, Jesus, Jesus } Grant us grace to love you

Jesus, grant us grace truly to love you for your great goodness and the generous gifts we have received, and hope always to receive from you.

Let the thought of your goodness and patience overcome our sinful inclinations.

Let the consideration of the times you have come into our lives to help and save us, make us ashamed of our ingratitude.

To think that you ask nothing of us in return, except that we should love you, and you ask that only because you are so good!

Dear Lord, our whole life shall be nothing but a desire for you, and to show our love we shall keep your commandments faithfully.

Have mercy on all sinners, Jesus, we beg you; turn their vices into virtues, convert their hearts to love of you and your commandments and bring them to bliss in everlasting glory.

Have mercy also on the souls in purgatory, for your bitter Passion, we beg you, and for your glorious name, Jesus. (Our Father . . . Hail Mary . . .)

from The Jesus Psalter

Let us love one another
since love comes from God
and everyone who loves is begotten by God and knows God . . .
No one has ever seen God;
but as long as we love one another
God will live in us
and his love will be complete in us . . .
God is love
and anyone who lives in love
lives in God,
and God lives in him.

1 John 4: 7–16

God loved the world so much
that he gave his only Son,
so that everyone who believes in him
may not be lost,
but may have eternal life.

John 3: 16

Where true love is dwelling, God is dwelling there;
Love's own loving presence love does ever share.

Love of Christ has made us out of many one;
In our midst is dwelling God's eternal Son.

Give him joyful welcome, love him and revere;
Cherish one another with a love sincere.

James Quinn

O heart of love, I put all my trust in thee. For I fear all things from my own weakness, but I hope for all things from thy goodness. St Margaret Mary

This is my commandment
love one another,
as I have loved you.

John 15: 12

Our love is not to be just words and mere talk,
but something real and active.

1 John 3: 18

For I am certain of this: neither death nor life, no angel, no prince, nothing that exists, nothing still to come, not any power, or height or depth, nor any created thing, can ever come between us and the love of God made visible in Christ Jesus our Lord.

Romans 8: 35–39

Arise, Lord! Redeem us because of your love.

Psalm 43 (44): 27

Jesus, grant me the grace to love you.
O blessed Jesu, make me love you entirely.
O blessed Jesu, let me deeply consider your love for me.
O blessed Jesu, give me the grace to thank you for your gifts.
Sweet Jesu, possess my heart, hold and keep it for yourself alone. St John Fisher

THE PRESENCE OF GOD

I will walk in the presence of the Lord
in the land of the living.

Psalm 114 (115): 9

Be still, and know that I am God.

Psalm 45 (46): 11

Where two or three meet in my name, I shall be there with them. Matthew 18: 20

If anyone loves me he will keep my word,
and my Father will love him,
and we shall come to him
and make our home with him.

John 14: 23

Alone with none but thee, my God,
I journey on my way;
What need I fear, when thou art near,
O King of night and day?
More safe am I within thy hand
Than if a host did round me stand.

St Columba

If anyone acknowledges that Jesus is the Son of God,
God lives in him and he in God. 1 John 4: 15

We are enfolded in the Father, we are enfolded in the Son, and we are enfolded in the Holy Spirit. And the Father is enfolded in us, and the Son is enfolded in us, and the Holy Spirit is enfolded in us.

Julian of Norwich

Lord, true light and creator of light,
grant that faithfully pondering on all that is holy,
we may ever live in the splendour of your presence.

Morning Prayer

O gracious and holy Father,
give us wisdom to perceive you,
intelligence to understand you,
diligence to seek you,
patience to wait for you,
eyes to behold you,
a heart to meditate upon you,
and a life to proclaim you;
through the power of the Spirit
of Jesus Christ our Lord.

St Benedict

God be in my head and in my understanding;
God be in mine eyes, and in my looking;
God be in my mouth, and in my speaking;
God be in my heart, and in my thinking;
God be at mine end, and at my departing.

Book of Hours, 1514

Glory be to him whose power, working in us, can do infinitely more than we can ask or imagine; glory be to him from generation to generation in the Church and in Christ Jesus for ever and ever. Amen.

Ephesians 3: 20–21

Through your faith, God's power will guard you until the salvation which has been prepared is revealed at the end of time. 1 Peter 1: 5

O God come to my aid,
O Lord make haste to help me!

Christ was crucified through weakness, and still he lives now through the power of God. So then, we are weak, as he was, but we shall live with him, through the power of God. 2 Corinthians 13: 4

My grace is enough for you: my power is at its best in weakness. 2 Corinthians 12: 9

The Lord's right hand has triumphed;
his right hand raised me.
The Lord's right hand has triumphed;
I shall not die, I shall live.
Psalm 117 (118): 16–17

It were my soul's desire
to see the face of God;
it were my soul's desire
to rest in his abode.

Grant, Lord, my soul's desire,
deep waves of cleansing sighs,
grant, Lord, my soul's desire,
from earthly cares to rise.

It were my soul's desire
to imitate my King,
it were my soul's desire
his endless praise to sing.

It were my soul's desire,
when heaven's gate is won,
to find my soul's desire
clear shining like the sun.

This still my soul's desire,
whatever life afford,
to gain my soul's desire,
and see thy face, O Lord.

CREATION

O Lord, how great are your works,
how wonderful are your designs.
Psalm 91 (92): 6

God saw all he had made, and indeed it was very good.
Genesis 1: 31

Long ago you founded the earth, Lord,
and the heavens are the work of your hands.
Psalm 101 (102): 26

Blessed are you, Lord, God of all creation.
Through your goodness we have ourselves to offer,
whom you have made and called to be your children.
May we live indeed as the work of your hands.
Blessed be God for ever.

The heavens proclaim the glory of God
and the firmament shows forth the work of his
hands.
Day unto day takes up the story
and night unto night makes known the message.

No speech, no word, no voice is heard
yet their span extends through all the earth,
their words to the utmost bounds of the world.

There he has placed a tent for the sun;
it comes forth like a bridegroom coming from his
tent,
rejoices like a champion to run its course.

At the end of the sky is the rising of the sun;
to the furthest end of the sky is its course.
There is nothing concealed from its burning heat.

Psalm 18 (19)

O thou, who art the true sun of the world, ever rising, and never going down; who by thy most wholesome appearing and sight dost nourish and gladden all things in heaven and earth; we beseech thee mercifully to shine into our hearts, that the night and darkness of sin, and the mists of error on every side, being driven away by the brightness of thy shining within our hearts, we may all our life walk without stumbling, as in the day time, and being pure and clean from the works of darkness, may abound in all good works which thou hadst prepared for us to walk in. Amen.

Erasmus

It was the Lord God who formed the mountains,
created the wind,
reveals his mind to man
makes both dawn and dark,
walks on the top of the heights of the world.

Amos 4: 13

PRAISE AND THANKSGIVING

My soul, give thanks to the Lord,
all my being, bless his holy name.
My soul, give thanks to the Lord,
and never forget all his blessings.
Psalm 102 (103): 1–2

O give thanks to the Lord for he is good;
for his love endures for ever.
Psalm 106 (107): 1

Let everything that lives and that breathes
give praise to the Lord. Psalm 150: 6

The Lord gave, the Lord has taken back. Blessed be the name of the Lord. Job 1: 21

Thanks be to you, my Lord Jesus Christ,
for all the benefits which you have given me,
for all the pains and insults
which you have borne for me.
O most merciful Redeemer, Friend and Brother,
may I know you more clearly,
love you more dearly,
follow you more nearly,
day by day. St Richard of Chichester

Let the message of Christ, in all its richness, find a home with you. Teach each other, and advise each other, in all wisdom. With gratitude in your hearts sing psalms and hymns and inspired songs to God; and never say or do anything except in the name of the Lord Jesus, giving thanks to God the Father through him. Colossians 3: 16–17

Whatever you eat, whatever you drink, whatever you do at all, do it for the glory of God.
1 Corinthians 10: 31

The Lord's is the earth and its fulness.
Come let us adore him!

Antiphon

Give thanks to the Lord for he is good,
for his love endures for ever.

Psalm 117 (118): 1

You are our Lord and our God, you are worthy of glory and honour and power, because you made all the universe and it was only by your will that everything was made and exists. Revelation 4: 11

How rich are the depths of God – how deep his wisdom and knowledge – and how impossible to penetrate his motives or understand his methods! Who could ever know the mind of the Lord? Who could ever be his counsellor? Who could ever give him anything or lend him anything? All that exists comes from him; all is by him and for him. To him be glory for ever! Amen.

Romans 11: 33–36

THE CHURCH

Jesus put another parable before them: 'The kingdom of heaven is like a mustard seed which a man took and sowed in his field. It is the smallest of all the seeds, but when it has grown it is the biggest shrub of all and becomes a tree so that the birds of the air come and shelter in its branches.'

He told them another parable: 'The kingdom of heaven is like the yeast a woman took and mixed in with three measures of flour till it was leavened all through.' . . .

And again: 'The kingdom of heaven is like treasure hidden in a field which someone has found; he hides it again, goes off happy, sells everything he owns and buys the field.

'Again, the Kingdom of heaven is like a merchant looking for fine pearls; when he finds one of great value he goes and sells everything he owns and buys it.

'Again, the kingdom of heaven is like a dragnet cast into the sea that brings in a haul of all kinds. When it is full, the fishermen haul it ashore; then, sitting down, they collect the good ones in a basket and throw away those that are no use.' Matthew 13: 31–49

Jesus said, 'You are Peter and upon this rock I will build my Church. And the gates of the underworld can never hold out against it. I will give you the keys of the kingdom of heaven; whatever you bind on earth shall be considered bound in heaven; whatever you loose on earth shall be considered loosed in heaven.'

Matthew 16: 18–19

They remained faithful to the teaching of the apostles, to the brotherhood, to the breaking of bread and to the prayers . . .

The faithful all lived together and owned everything in common; they sold their goods and possessions and shared out the proceeds amongst themselves according to what each needed.

They went as a body to the temple every day but met in their houses for the breaking of the bread; they shared their food gladly and generously; they praised God and were looked up to by everyone. Day by day the Lord added to their community those destined to be saved. Acts 2: 42–47

You shall be my people. I will be your God.

Ezekiel 36: 28

You are a chosen race, a royal priesthood, a consecrated nation, a people set apart to sing the praises of God who called you out of darkness into his wonderful light. Once you were not a people at all and now you are the People of God. 1 Peter 2: 9–10

May your Church, Lord, be a light to the nations, the sign and source of your power to unite all men. May she lead mankind to the mystery of your love.

Bidding Prayer

FREEDOM

The Law, of course, as we all know, is spiritual; but I am unspiritual; I have been sold as a slave to sin. I cannot understand my own behaviour. I fail to carry out the things I want to do, and I find myself doing the very things I hate. When I act against my own will, that means I have a self that acknowledges that the Law is good, and so the thing behaving in that way is not my self but sin living in me. The fact is, I know of nothing good living in me – living, that is, in my unspiritual self – for though the will to do what is good is in me, the performance is not, with the result that instead of doing the good things I want to do, I carry out the sinful things I do not want. When I act against my will, then, it is not my true self doing it, but sin which lives in me. In fact, this seems to be the rule, that every single time I want to do good it is something evil that comes to hand. In my inmost self I dearly love God's Law, but I can see that my body dictates a different law that battles against the law which my reason dictates. This is what makes me a prisoner of that law of sin which lives inside my body. What a wretched man I am! Who will rescue me from this body doomed to death? Thanks be to God through Jesus Christ our Lord!

Romans 7: 14–25

The man who looks steadily at the perfect law of freedom and makes that his habit – not listening and then forgetting, but actively putting it into practice – will be happy in all that he does.

James 1: 25

You, Lord, are the source of our freedom. Bring those in captivity of mind or body to the freedom of the children of God. Bidding Prayer

If the Son makes you free,
you will be free indeed.

John 8: 36

A slave, when he is called in the Lord, becomes the Lord's freedman, and a freeman called in the Lord becomes Christ's slave. 1 Corinthians 7: 22

If in union with Christ we have imitated his death, we shall also imitate him in his resurrection. We must realise that our former selves have been crucified with him to destroy this sinful body and to free us from the slavery of sin. When a man dies, of course, he has finished with sin. Romans 6: 5–7

If you make my word your own
you will indeed be my disciples,
you will learn the truth
and the truth will make you free.

John 8: 31–32

All baptised in Christ, you have all clothed yourselves in Christ, and there are no more distinctions between Jew and Greek, slave and free, male and female, but all of you are one in Christ Jesus.

Galatians 3: 27–28

You are slaves of no one except God, so behave like free men, and never use your freedom as an excuse for wickedness. Have respect for everyone and love for our community.

1 Peter 2: 16–17

Everyone moved by the Spirit is a son of God. The spirit you received is not the spirit of slaves bringing fear into your lives again; it is the spirit of sons, and it makes us cry out, 'Abba, Father!' The Spirit himself and our spirit bear united witness that we are children of God. And if we are children we are heirs as well: heirs of God and coheirs with Christ, sharing his sufferings so as to share his glory.

Romans 8: 14–17

The spirit of the Lord has been given to me,
for he has anointed me.
He has sent me to bring the good news to the poor,
to proclaim liberty to captives
and to the blind new sight,
to set the downtrodden free,
to proclaim the Lord's year of favour.

Isaiah 61: 1–2

Night Prayer

We end the day as we began it, by remembering God's presence.

In the name of the Father,
and of the Son,
and of the Holy Spirit. Amen.

Save us, Lord, while we are awake;
protect us while we sleep;
that we may keep watch with Christ
and rest with him in peace.

God has been with us throughout the day, but there may have been moments when we forgot his love and turned from him. We may pray for forgiveness:

Turn your ear, O Lord, and give answer
for I am poor and needy.
Preserve my life, for I am faithful:
save the servant who trusts in you.

You are my God, have mercy on me, Lord,
for I cry to you all the day long.
Give joy to your servant, O Lord,
for to you I lift up my soul.

O Lord, you are good and forgiving,
full of love to all who call.
Give heed, O Lord, to my prayer
and attend to the sound of my voice.

In the day of distress I will call
and surely you will reply.

Psalm 85 (86): 1–7

He will always reply, but he asks us to know ourselves so that we may grow in holiness. Pause for a moment to see how you have lived today. (There is an examination of conscience based on St Paul's portrait of love on p. 170.)

A prayer of sorrow

Lord God, our loving Father,
you know all my sins and failures,
my weaknesses and temptations.
I come to you with deep sorrow in my heart
for the wrong I have done and for the good I have failed to do.
Forgive me, accept me, and strengthen me,
now and always. Amen.

A traditional prayer of sorrow

My God, I am sorry and ask forgiveness for my sins.
By the help of your grace I will try not to sin again.

There are many wonderful prayers of sorrow among the Psalms; see especially Psalm 50 (51).

Despite any failures there may have been today, it will have been a day, like every day, marked by God's care and blessing. Remember quietly the good moments – the success, the happiness, the laughter, the peacefulness – and give thanks to God for them.

* Lord, I thank you for all you have done for me today.
Help me to see you more clearly in my life.

* Remember, Lord, all those I love.
Teach me to be more generous towards them.

* Stay close, Lord, to those who have been with me today.
Comfort those whom I have harmed;
forgive those who may have hurt me;
bless those who have encouraged me.

* May the work I have done today, Lord,
give glory to you
and be of service to my neighbour.

A prayer of happiness and peace.

Preserve me, God, I take refuge in you.
I say to the Lord: 'You are my God.
My happiness lies in you alone.'

O Lord, it is you who are my portion and cup;
it is you yourself who are my prize.
The lot marked out for me is my delight:
welcome indeed the heritage that falls to me!

I will bless the Lord who gives me counsel,
who even at night directs my heart.

I keep the Lord ever in my sight;
since he is at my right hand, I shall stand firm.

And so my heart rejoices, my soul is glad;
even my body shall rest in safety.
You will show me the path of life,
the fulness of joy in your presence,
at your right hand happiness for ever.

from Psalm 15 (16)

There is a time to pray for the peace that comes at the end of life:

May the Lord support us all the day long,
till the shades lengthen and the evening comes,
and the busy world is hushed,
and the fever of life is over,
and our work is done.
Then in his mercy
may he give us a safe lodging,
and a holy rest,
and peace at the last. Amen.

Cardinal Newman

As we end the day we can remember again that we belong to the whole family of the saints, and ask Mary, our mother, to pray for us:

Hail, Holy Queen, Mother of Mercy!
Hail, our life, our sweetness and our hope.
To you do we cry, poor banished children of Eve;
to you do we send up our sighs,
mourning and weeping in this vale of tears.
Turn, then, most gracious advocate,
your eyes of mercy towards us;
and after this our exile,
show unto us the blessed fruit of your womb,
Jesus.
O clement, O loving, O sweet Virgin Mary.

May the Lord grant me a quiet night,
and a perfect end. Amen.

A Meditation on the Mysteries of the Rosary

The Joyful Mysteries

THE ANNUNCIATION

The angel Gabriel was sent by God to a town in Galilee called Nazareth, to a virgin betrothed to a man named Joseph, and the virgin's name was Mary. He went in and said to her, 'Rejoice, so highly favoured! The Lord is with you. You are to conceive and bear a son, and you must name him Jesus. He will be great and will be called Son of the Most High.' Mary said to the angel, 'But how can this come about, since I am a virgin?' 'The Holy Spirit will come upon you' the angel answered, 'and the power of the Most High will cover you with its shadow. And so the child will be holy and will be called Son of God.' 'I am the handmaid of the Lord,' said Mary 'let what you have said be done to me.' And the angel left her.

from Luke 1: 26–38

What a frightening invitation, to become mother of
such a child . . .
a child of infinite promise.
One can imagine the sudden clutch of fear . . .
the puzzlement . . .
the anxiety about the future.
Surely he doesn't really mean me?
But in a moment the fears are stilled,
and all is seen to be possible.
'Be it done to me according to your word.'

What is my annunciation? When has God sent his angel to me to announce his Good News? And how have I reacted to the promises he has made to me?

God's messengers do come to me;
they tell me that I'm highly favoured . . .
much graced and blessed . . .
with much fruit to bear . . .
and they tell me too that the Lord is with me.

But often I do not recognise God's friends,
because their words are so demanding,
and I am afraid.

Everyone is blessed by God . . .
he has no favourites.
God is with all his people . . .
he cannot forget any one of them.
All are chosen people . . .
each one unique . . .
every person special.
'Do not be afraid,' he says to me 'for I have redeemed you; I have called you by your name and you are mine.'

I have been called by God to do him some definite service . . .
I have a vocation to become what he calls me to be.
If I am ever to answer this call
I must learn to say,
'Yes . . . Let it be done . . . Let it be done . . .
Let it be done to me according to your word.'

I must let go –
of fear . . .
of a sense of inadequacy . . .
of selfishness and pride . . .
of wanting to have everything planned before I make a move.
Then I may learn to trust in God; who is Father, Friend, Tremendous Lover; who knows what I can do; and to whom nothing is impossible.

Speak, Lord, your servant hears!

THE VISITATION

> Mary set out and went as quickly as she could to a town in the hill country of Judah. She went to Zechariah's house and greeted Elizabeth. Now as soon as Elizabeth heard Mary's greeting, the child leapt in her womb and Elizabeth was filled with the Holy Spirit. She gave a loud cry and said, 'Of all women you are the most blessed, and blessed is the fruit of your womb. Why should I be honoured with a visit from the mother of my Lord? For the moment your greeting reached my ears, the child in my womb leapt for joy. Yes, blessed is she who believed that the promise made her by the Lord would be fulfilled.' Mary stayed with Elizabeth about three months and then went back home. Luke 1: 39–45, 56

It is a sign of generosity to be willing to share in another's happiness. Mary's first thought after the angel had left her was to visit her cousin Elizabeth, who 'in her old age had herself conceived a son'.

There was respect in this visit . . .
also thoughtfulness . . .
and a certain delicacy.

Elizabeth was an older woman . . . perhaps she was unsure of the future . . . she must have welcomed the help and companionship . . . all Mary could give were her time and herself . . . gifts that really count.

The generous gift brings a heartfelt response:
'Blessed is she who believed
that the promise made her by the Lord
would be fulfilled.'

This is another Beatitude:
I am really blessed if I believe
in the love of God, which enfolds me . . .

in the truth of his Word, which speaks to me . . .
in the power of his Spirit, which overshadows me.
Then I shall know that the 'Almighty has done great things for me', and that I shall live for ever.

First, though, I have to believe in others . . .
and this means that I must visit them and meet them –
not just casually in the hairdresser's, or the pub, or the office or factory, or on the doorstep,
where all we talk about is football, the weather, cars or the way prices are rising . . .
but generously, so as to take them into my heart . . .
and share with them something of myself.

This is hard to do . . .
I have been taught to protect myself with
my privacy . . .
my shyness . . .
my self-imposed loneliness . . .
my property.

If only I can take the risk
to be open to others . . .
to be patient with them . . .
to waste time with them . . .
to listen to them,
then I shall learn to believe in them, and they to believe in me.

This takes time . . . more even than three months . . . and love . . . but the reward is God himself . . . for God is love.

Teach me, Lord, to give myself generously for others.

THE BIRTH OF OUR LORD

Joseph travelled up to Bethlehem to be registered together with Mary, his betrothed, who was with child. While they were there the time came for her to have her child, and she gave birth to a son, her first-born. She wrapped him in swaddling clothes, and laid him in a manger because there was no room for them at the inn. The angel of the Lord appeared to some shepherds close by, and said, 'Today in the town of David a saviour has been born to you; he is Christ the Lord.' The shepherds said to one another, 'Let us go to Bethlehem and see this thing that has happened which the Lord has made known to us.' So they hurried away and found Mary and Joseph, and the baby lying in the manger, and they went back glorifying and praising God for all they had heard and seen.

The Word was made flesh,
he lived among us.

from Luke 2: 1–20; John 1: 14

Every birth is truly a miracle. Each birth marks God's entry into the world. A new-born child is made in the image of God, he is made for God, and he is only fully alive when he knows God as his Father in heaven.

This birth is the perfect sign that God is with us.
God has spoken.
His Word has been given to the world.

This is a mystery to ponder . . .
a wonder to marvel at . . .
a glory to sing about.
'Glory to God in the highest, and peace to his people on earth.'

It scarcely seems credible that this child,
born in such simplicity . . .
recognised by only a handful of shepherds . . .
should be Saviour . . . Son of God . . . God-with-us . . .

the Image of the invisible God . . .
the last revelation of God to man.

But so he is.

I need to understand that God reveals himself to the
poor and simple . . .
that it is the ordinary things of life –
a smile, a word;
forgiveness, freedom;
life itself and the whole of creation –
which show the grandeur of God . . .
that it is because he was born in poverty and simplicity that I have the courage to approach him, for he is like me in all things except sin.

Many of my friends are searching for God, but perhaps I do not show them where to look for him, or how to recognise him. Unwittingly I may have become a barrier to their faith,
by my unwillingness to talk about God . . .
by my ignorance of the Gospel message . . .
by my empty materialism.

What my friends are looking for is often so simple . . .
so ordinary . . . and so human,
that I have not grasped that their search is truly
for God, the Word made flesh.

Let me try to become a better witness to God's
presence,
to see him in the world he has made . . .
to meet him in my fellow men . . .
to know him through his eternal Word . . .
and so to proclaim him by my daily living.

May Christ be born in me today.

THE PRESENTATION

Mary and Joseph took Jesus up to Jerusalem to present him to the Lord. When they brought in the child Jesus to do for him what the Law required, Simeon took him into his arms and blessed God; and he said:

'Now my eyes have seen the salvation
which you have prepared for all the nations to see,
a light to enlighten the pagans
and the glory of your people Israel.'

He said to Mary, 'This child is destined to be a sign that is rejected – and a sword will pierce your own soul too.'

The Word was the true light
that enlightens all men.
He came to his own domain
and his own people did not accept him.

from Luke 2: 22–35; John 1: 9, 11

All belongs to God. He is the Creator. Everything comes from him and in due course returns to him. 'Every good and perfect gift comes from above, from the Father of all light.' Mary and Joseph knew that their wonderful gift was from God . . . and must be brought back to him. Simeon saw that the child would dispel the world's darkness . . . though through suffering and rejection.

What child is this?
His parents could not see into the future . . .
could not know the life he would lead . . .
or the death he would suffer . . .
could not imagine the richness of the one in their care.
They knew he was called by God,
and so they did for him what God's Law required.

Of any infant we may ask, 'What child is this?'.
We can never fathom the mystery of another . . .
or know his future . . .
or map his journey.

All we know for certain is that he is called by God and that we who have care for him must do as God's Law requires.

We may learn from God:
'When you were a child I loved you.
I myself taught you to walk,
I took you in my arms;
I led you with reins of kindness,
with leading-strings of love.'
This is the Law . . . to love.

What is God's plan for me?
'In God's plan
every single man is called upon to grow.
Each life is a vocation.
From birth, each one of us carries within himself
the seeds of personal growth.
Each one of us can bear the fruit
proposed for him by God.'

Like Christ, I am called to enlighten the world, and so must be ready,
to be rejected . . .
to be misunderstood . . .
to suffer hardship for justice's sake . . .
to be without honour among my own people.

I must first be pruned . . . bear much fruit . . . and so return to God enriched.

O Lord be praised for what I am, and what I may become!

THE FINDING IN THE TEMPLE

Every year his parents used to go to Jerusalem for the feast of the Passover. When he was twelve years old, they went up for the feast as usual. When they were on their way home after the feast, the boy Jesus stayed behind in Jerusalem without his parents knowing it. Three days later, they found him in the Temple, sitting among the doctors, listening to them, and asking them questions; and all those who heard him were astounded at his intelligence and his replies. They were overcome when they saw him, and his mother said to him, 'My child, why have you done this to us? See how worried your father and I have been, looking for you.' 'Why were you looking for me?' he replied 'Did you not know that I must be busy with my Father's affairs?' But they did not understand what he meant. He then went down with them and came to Nazareth and lived under their authority. His mother stored up all these things in her heart. And Jesus increased in wisdom, in stature, and in favour with God and men. Luke 2: 41–43, 46–52

At first sight the incident is inexplicable. It is uncharacteristic . . . it seems to show thoughtlessness and even selfishness. But perhaps it can help me to realise how necessary it is

to let another grow . . .
to encourage him to be independent . . .
to give him room to be free . . .
to offer care without constraint . . .
to understand commitment to what is important . . .
to be ready always to listen to the questions being asked.

Jesus was a boy. Like all young people he needed to know himself . . . to find himself . . . and to become in his humanity what his Father was calling him to be. 'Did you not know that I must be busy with my Father's affairs? . . . My meat is to do the will of my Father in heaven.'

He listened and questioned.
There is a model for me.

What are the right questions for me to ask? Even to know the questions, I must first listen to God
in prayer . . .
in the words of scripture . . .
in the Church's teaching . . .
in the advice of God's friends . . .
in the wonder of his creation . . .
in the voice of conscience.
As I listen, so I shall learn to question well.

Jesus grew 'in wisdom, in stature, and in favour with God and men'.
This is my ambition, too – to grow.
Let me realise that
while God gives the increase,
I myself have a part to play
so that growth may be possible.

I need
to be open to the Holy Spirit, so I may repent and be converted . . .
to take proper care of myself, so I may have the energy to do God's work . . .
to be willing to know others, so I may meet the risen, living Christ . . .
to take time to ponder God's word, so I may learn true wisdom.

Then I will come to know myself . . . to find myself . . . and to become what the Father is calling me to be.

Lord, give me the patience to grow.

The Sorrowful Mysteries

THE AGONY IN THE GARDEN

When the Passover meal was over, Jesus left to make his way as usual to the Mount of Olives, to a small estate called Gethsemane, with the disciples following. Then he withdrew from them, about a stone's throw away, and knelt down and prayed. 'Father', he said, 'if you are willing take this cup away from me. Nevertheless, let your will be done, not mine.' Then an angel appeared to him, coming from heaven to give him strength. In his anguish he prayed even more earnestly, and his sweat fell to the ground like great drops of blood. When he rose from prayer he went to the disciples and found them sleeping for sheer grief. 'Why are you asleep?' he said to them. 'Get up and pray not to be put to the test.'

Luke 22: 39–46

Why didn't Jesus escape from his enemies? Was there any need for him to go through all this? Could he not have left quietly until the commotion had died down? This is the temptation that comes to us all at one time or another.

to avoid the issue . . .
to choose the easy way out . . .
to run away from what is right . . .

But there are some problems that simply have to be faced.

The cup has to be drained . . . the burden must be carried . . .

the needs of others must take first place.

Jesus, like us, prayed that he could be spared . . . he was in an agony of apprehension and fear so that he sweated blood. His prayer was answered: 'Not my will, but yours be done'.

In my agony, let this become my prayer.

In the agony
  of frustration, when it seems there is nothing I can do to ease the situation . . .
  of being misunderstood, when it's as if the whole world has turned its back on me . . .
  of shame, when my sins and failures overshadow the whole of life . . .
  of anxiety, when my responsibilities seem too great for me to bear . . .
  of apprehension, when the oncoming horror is too dreadful for me to face . . .
  of sadness, when someone I love turns against me and friendship dies . . .

Indeed I may pray not to be put to the test, and to be spared from such pain. But there are times when
  as a result of sin . . .
  or error . . .
  or accident . . .
  or sickness . . .
  or because of human weakness and limitation . . .
  or because of what my neighbour needs,
I shall undergo a fearful agony.

Then may I pray that I can know and accept God's will.

Lord, the spirit is willing, but the flesh is weak!

THE SCOURGING AT THE PILLAR

Pilate said to the chief priests and the elders, 'What am I to do with Jesus who is called Christ?' They all said, 'Let him be crucified!' 'Why?' he asked 'What harm has he done? He has done nothing that deserves death, so I shall have him flogged and let him go.' But they shouted all the louder, 'Let him be crucified!' Then Pilate saw that he was making no impression, that in fact a riot was imminent. So he took some water, washed his hands in front of the crowd and said, 'I am innocent of this man's blood. It is your concern.' He ordered Jesus to be first scourged and then handed over to be crucified.

from Matthew 27: 21–26; Luke 23: 15

When people are frightened there is no depth to which they won't sink. The chief priests were frightened because

Jesus was prepared to take the law into his own hands: 'the sabbath was made for man, not man for the sabbath' . . .

Jesus was popular with the ordinary people: 'his teaching made a deep impression on them because, unlike the scribes, he taught them with authority' . . .

Pilate was frightened because

Jesus was an enigma, whose kingdom was 'not of this world' . . .

Jesus bore witness to the truth, and the truth is uncomfortable for those whose lives are a lie . . .

So the Jews demanded his death, and Pilate looked for a compromise.

'He has done nothing that deserves death, so I shall have him flogged' . . . a sop to the Establishment . . . a ruthless injustice . . . 'it is expedient that one man should die for the people'.

How often are we prepared to allow an injustice because,
it is too much trouble to do anything about it . . .
we don't have the power to effect a worthwhile change . . .
we accept the law as our first obligation . . .
we are afraid to accept the truth . . .
material affairs outweigh the spiritual.
We pass by on the other side of the road, and avert our eyes.

Let me remember the pain endured by so many of my fellow men,
the distress of the sick; who look for my presence . . .
the suffering of the handicapped; who wait for my visits . . .
the timidity of the lonely; who hope for my friendship . . .
the anguish of the starving; who trust for my bread . . .
the heartache of the homeless; whose future looks so empty . . .
the emptiness of the sad; whose happiness is in my hands . . .
the despair of the falsely imprisoned; who plead for my help . . .

'Behold, the man!'

Jesus, the suffering one,
is present in all those who suffer,
and I, if I have faith, have the power to heal them.

Lord, give me the strength to bind up broken hearts.

THE CROWNING WITH THORNS

The governor's soldiers took Jesus with them. Then they stripped him and made him wear a scarlet cloak, and having twisted some thorns into a crown they put this on his head and placed a reed in his right hand. To make fun of him they knelt to him saying, 'Hail, king of the Jews!' And they spat on him and took the reed and struck him on the head with it. Matthew 27: 27–30

Mockery is often more hurtful than the hurt that attends it.

When Jesus Christ was yet a child
He had a garden small and wild,
Wherein he cherished roses fair,
And wove them into garlands there.

Now once, as summer-time drew nigh,
There came a troop of children by,
And seeing roses on the tree,
With shouts they plucked them merrily.

'Do you bind roses in your hair?'
They cried, in scorn, to Jesus there.
The boy said humbly: 'Take, I pray,
All but the naked thorns away.'

Then of the thorns they made a crown,
And with rough fingers pressed it down,
Till on his forehead fair and young
Red drops of blood like roses sprung.

Plechtcheev

I know it's not a perfect world and that envy, jealousy and hatred can be found everywhere:

'a sour suspicion born of fear that the other man is finer . . .

a subtle rumour breeding news that another's love is sweeter . . .
a tangled knowledge canker-grown that the stranger's path is straighter . . .
a numb awareness vainly fought that the weaker man's my leader.'
These, maybe, are the thorns in my crown.

But I do have a crown of roses . . . as well as thorns. My crown is woven of
my friends, whose constancy and love urge me to generosity . . .
my faith, a grace from God which tugs at me to know him . . .
my forgiveness, a sign of God's love that confirms my hope . . .

Wearing such a crown I may learn
to soften the thorns of selfishness . . .
to be happy with the gifts I have received . . .
to rejoice in the talents and success of others.

'Glory to God in the highest, and peace to his people on earth.'

THE CARRYING OF THE CROSS

Pilate handed Jesus over to the Jews to be crucified. They then took charge of him, and carrying his own cross he went out of the city to the place of the skull or, as it was called in Hebrew, Golgotha. As they were leading him away they seized on a man, Simon from Cyrene, who was coming in from the country, and made him shoulder the cross and carry it behind Jesus. Large numbers of people followed him, and of women, too, who mourned and lamented for him. But Jesus turned on them and said, 'Daughters of Jerusalem, do not weep for me; weep rather for yourselves and for your children.'

John 19: 17; Luke 23: 26–28

This was Jesus's last pilgrimage. His life had been marked by journeys:
the flight to Egypt . . .
the visit as a child to Jerusalem . . .
and later his missionary journeys to all parts of Palestine to tell his fellow countrymen about his Father.
Calvary was to be the final staging post.

He had told his followers,
'Take up your cross daily and follow me' . . .
'Come to me all you who labour and are over-burdened, and I will refresh you' . . .
'My yoke is easy and my burden light'.

It is said that the condemned prisoner carried only the cross piece, which was lashed to his arms . . . the vertical post stayed in position at the top of the hill.

The horizontal – a reminder
that like Christ I am on a pilgrim journey . . .
that like Christ I cannot always choose the way . . .
that like Christ I carry with me a burden I cannot lose . . .

The vertical – a reminder
that God is always there . . .
that all I do is in the end to give him glory . . .
that my journey to heaven must be rooted in the ground . . .

If my life is really a pilgrimage to God, carrying the weight of myself, it is sensible
to abandon unnecessary trifles so as not to be encumbered
for I cannot serve God and material things . . .
to be willing to lay the axe to the root of the tree and be converted,
for to be perfect is to have changed often . . .
to accept the company of others, their consolation and their help,
for on my own I am powerless . . .
The road is rough and the falls are many.

God draws me towards himself, for
his love is patient . . .
my baptism has marked me out for him . . .
my heart knows no rest until it rests in him.

Lord, see that I do not follow the wrong path
and lead me in the path of life eternal.

THE CRUCIFIXION

When they reached the place called The Skull, they crucified him there and the two criminals also, one on the right, the other on the left. Jesus said, 'Father forgive them; they do not know what they are doing'. Then they cast lots to share out his clothing. When the sixth hour came there was darkness over the whole land until the ninth hour. And at the ninth hour Jesus cried out in a loud voice, 'My God, my God, why have you deserted me?' Then he said, 'Father, into your hands I commit my spirit'. With these words he breathed his last. When the centurion saw what had taken place, he gave praise to God and said, 'This was a great and good man'. And when all the people who had gathered for the spectacle saw what had happened, they went home beating their breasts. All his friends stood at a distance; so also did the women who had accompanied him from Galilee, and they saw all this happen.

Luke 23: 33–34, 46–49; Mark 15: 33–34

Death is inescapable, but this does not make it any the less frightening. Jesus himself was afraid, and even felt for a time that he had been forgotten by his Father. There can be no worse horror than believing ourselves to have been abandoned. Such an experience can come to anyone, when

God, and faith in God seem to have vanished . . .
friends stand at a distance, and don't want to know us . . .
all those we have relied on for support suddenly have nothing to offer . . .

At moments like this I must remind myself that dying should be a daily experience if the last enemy, death itself, is to be conquered.
Jesus said:

'Unless the wheat grain falls on the ground and dies
it remains only a single grain

but if it dies
it yields a rich harvest . . .
Anyone who finds his life will lose it;
anyone who loses his life for my sake will find it . . .'

If I am to learn the art of living, I must practise the art of dying. 'Death is swallowed up in victory' . . . it is a threshold to new life.

To die is to let go,
of prejudices, vanities and my own opinion . . .
of those ambitions that turn me from what is worthwhile . . .
of the things, the comforts and even the people who distract me from God . . .

To die is to become obedient,
to God's commandments . . .
to the needs of others . . .
to the demands of the present moment . . .

To die is to empty myself . . . to belong to others . . . to cast aside the inessential . . . to leave something to God . . . to abandon myself: 'Father, into your hands I commit my spirit'.

At death there are no more tomorrows . . . but only a memory of yesterdays . . . and an eternal present.

Then I shall truly know that God has not forgotten me, and that I am safe in his hands.

Lord, teach me how to die.

The Glorious Mysteries

THE RESURRECTION

On the first day of the week, at the first sign of dawn, the women went to the tomb with the spices they had prepared. They found that the stone had been rolled away from the tomb, but on entering discovered that the body of the Lord Jesus was not there. As they stood there not knowing what to think, two men in brilliant clothes suddenly appeared at their side. Terrified, the women lowered their eyes. But the two men said to them, 'Why look among the dead for someone who is alive?' He is not here; he has risen. Remember what he told you when he was still in Galilee: that the Son of Man had to be handed over into the power of sinful men and be crucified, and rise again on the third day?' And they remembered his words. Luke 24: 1–8

The apostles were, to our way of thinking, slow to believe the full message of the Gospel. 'Did you not know,' the risen Christ said to the despondent couple on the road to Emmaus 'that the Christ had to suffer and so enter into his glory?'

Wake up from your sleep
rise from the dead
and Christ will shine on you.

He died,
so that his Father might raise him to a new life . . .
so that all of us could be brought alive in Christ.
St Paul says, 'If Christ is not risen our faith is in vain'.

Let me notice the small reminders in my ordinary life that point the way to a richer life with God . . . and give thanks to him for
the simple pleasure of food and drink . . .
the security of shelter and home . . .
the tranquillity of sleep and quiet . . .

Let me appreciate the emergence of new life that is a daily miracle for all its frequency and inevitability . . . and praise God for
the coming to birth of a new day . . .
the beauty produced by the work of human hands . . .
the recovery of strength after sickness . . .
and above all, the birth of a child . . .

Let me marvel at the brief resurrections I experience in my struggle to follow Christ . . . and thank God for
forgiveness, after failure and sin . . .
praise, when all I had expected was to be unnoticed . . .
trust, when I knew it was undeserved . . .
welcome, in spite of my selfish isolation.

All of this is an anticipation and promise of what is to come . . . which eye has not seen . . . nor ear heard . . . which has not entered into the heart of man.

If I want to be alive I must 'eat the flesh of the Son of Man and drink his blood' . . . I must do as he did . . . in memory of him. My communion with him at Mass is the perfect foretaste of what is to come and the source of the resurrection I must search for:
The Sacred Banquet
in which Christ is received . . .
the memory of his Passion recalled . . .
the mind filled with grace . . .
and a pledge of future glory given.

'Lord, that I may live, and live to the full!'

THE ASCENSION

May the God of our Lord Jesus Christ, the Father of glory, give you a spirit of wisdom and perception of what is revealed, to bring you to full knowledge of him. May he enlighten the eyes of your mind so that you can see what hope his call holds for you, what rich glories he has promised the saints will inherit and how infinitely great is the power that he has exercised for us believers. This you can tell from the strength of his power at work in Christ, when he used it to raise him from the dead and to make him sit at his right hand, in heaven. He has put all things under his feet, and made for him, as the ruler of everything, the head of the Church; which is his body, the fullness of him who fills the whole creation.

Jesus said to the apostles, 'All authority in heaven and on earth has been given to me. Go, therefore, make disciples of all the nations; baptise them in the name of the Father and of the Son and of the Holy Spirit, and teach them to observe all the commands I gave you. And know that I am with you always; yes, to the end of time.'

Ephesians 1: 17–23; Matthew 28: 18–20

Jesus is now with his Father . . . continually interceding on our behalf. But he is alive too in all the members of his Body, the Church . . . he fills them with his own life . . . he encourages, forgives, guides . . . he helps the whole of creation to achieve its purpose.

The Master Craftsman has given his apprentices all he can . . . it is for them now, under his care, to continue his work . . . to witness . . . to heal . . . to set free those who are enslaved. Much has been entrusted to us.

I'm scared of such great responsibility,
'You can't mean me to do this, Lord' . . .
'Lord, I am not worthy' . . .
'I do not know how to speak, Lord: I'm only a child' . . .

I want to hide and leave it to those who are better fitted: the bishops . . . the priests . . . the nuns . . . the clever ones . . . the holy ones. And all he says to me is
'Do not be afraid, for I have redeemed you . . .
I have called you by your name . . .
and you are mine.'

I am part of the body of Christ . . . there are all sorts of service to be done . . . but it is the same God who is working in all of them . . . I cannot say 'Christ has no need of me' . . . my place, my work, my mission are indispensable . . . I need not be fainthearted, because Jesus Christ is working in me . . . with him all things are possible.

I must be ready then to be a witness to the power of Christ in me,
by hearing his word and keeping it . . .
by making his teaching my own . . .
by spreading the Gospel by word and action . . .
by practising justice and integrity . . .
by readiness to take up my cross daily . . .
by faithfulness to my daily prayer . . .

If he is on my side . . . I have nothing to fear.

My witness may be silent . . . but it will be nonetheless strong and effective.

'O Lord, open my lips;
and my tongue shall announce your praise!'

THE COMING OF THE HOLY SPIRIT

I shall ask the Father, and he will give you another Advocate to be with you for ever. The Advocate, the Holy Spirit, whom the Father will send in my name, will teach you everything and remind you of all I have said to you. When the Spirit of truth comes he will lead you to the complete truth.

When Pentecost day came round, they had all met in one room, when suddenly they heard what sounded like a powerful wind from heaven, the noise of which filled the entire house in which they were sitting; and something appeared to them that seemed like tongues of fire; these separated and came to rest on the head of each of them. They were all filled with the Holy Spirit, and began to speak foreign languages as the Spirit gave them the gift of speech. John 14: 16, 26; 16: 23; Acts 2: 1–4

God's mystery is gradually unfolded. He is Father . . . the Creator . . . the one who holds all things in being . . . the Shepherd of his people . . . the Bridegroom.

He is Son . . . the Son of God made man . . . the Word made flesh . . . the image of the invisible God . . . who died so that we might live.

He is Holy Spirit . . . sent by the Father and the Son . . . Advocate . . . Helper . . . Breath of Life . . . who comes to everyone who invites him. The Spirit of God is man's partner . . . he enobles . . . teaches . . . directs.

The gifts of the Spirit cannot be counted . . . they are as many as there are people in the world, and more besides . . . but among them we can number,

the wisdom of the man who knows real worth when he finds it . . .

the understanding of a mother who can reach her daughter's heart . . .

the judgement of the youngster who reads a situation with uncomplicated simplicity . . .
the courage of the one who is prepared to swim against the stream . . .
the knowledge of the man of prayer whose faith and peace are unshakeable . . .
the unfathomable respect of a son for his father, and of a father for his son . . .

The cheerfulness of the dying . . . the generosity of the poor . . . the angry fire of the prophet . . . the patience of the teacher . . . the smile of a friend . . . the sorrow of a sinner . . . the compassion of the one who forgives.

The disciples of Jesus were dispirited . . . they had lost heart . . . the bottom had dropped out of their lives . . . the urgency of the gospel had disappeared . . . they were filled with fear. 'What can we do?' . . . 'Is God still with us?' . . . 'What will happen to us?' . . .

Then the Spirit came and all was changed. They were enlivened . . . inspired . . . encouraged . . . renewed. They were eager with the fire of unselfish love . . . alive with the rhythm of a new beginning . . . confident in the discovery of truth.

I must look for my personal Pentecost . . . ready to accept the Spirit when he comes . . . willing to be converted . . . happy to abandon myself to his urgent leadership . . . so that there may grow in me the Christian instinct for truth . . . love . . . joy . . . peace . . . patience . . . kindness . . . goodness . . . trustfulness . . . gentleness . . . self-control.

'Come, O Holy Spirit and kindle in me the fire of your love.'

THE ASSUMPTION

Christ has in fact been raised from the dead, the first-fruits of all who have fallen asleep. Death came through one man and in the same way the resurrection of the dead has come through one man. Just as all men die in Adam, so all men will be brought to life in Christ; but all of them in their proper order: Christ as the first-fruits and then, after the coming of Christ, those who belong to him.

God loved us with so much love that he was generous with his mercy: when we were dead through our sins, he brought us to life with Christ – it is through grace that you have been saved – and raised us up with him and gave us a place with him in heaven, in Christ Jesus. This was to show for all ages to come, through his goodness towards us in Christ Jesus, how infinitely rich he is in grace. Because it is by grace that you have been saved, through faith; not by anything of your own, but by a gift from God; not by anything that you have done, so that nobody can claim the credit. We are God's work of art, created in Christ Jesus to live the good life as from the beginning he had meant us to live it.

1 Corinthians 15: 20–23; Ephesians 2: 4–10

In a very special way Mary is God's work of art.
Alone of creation she lived the good life
as from the beginning she was called by God to live it.

Like all works of art she was irreplaceable . . . indestructible . . . incorruptible. She was unscathed and untouched by the sin of the world that she lived in . . . she knew not sin . . . and so conquered the one who fathers death.

Mary immaculate, star of the morning,
chosen before the creation began,
chosen to bring, for your bridal adorning,
woe to the serpent and rescue to man.

She was chosen to be
  the mother of the Lord . . . who would triumph over sin and death;
  the second Eve . . . bringing not death but life to men;
  the new mother of Mankind . . . taking all into her heart.
After her Son – 'the first-fruits of all who have fallen asleep' – she was brought to life in Christ. It was by God's grace that she was saved, for all are given life by God's free gift.

She was full of grace . . . supremely free to choose . . . wholly willing to walk the passage of earthly life to the incomparable life of glory.

In my daily life I have
  to struggle against temptation . . .
  to endure the suffering that comes to everyone . . .
  to bring woe to the serpent and rescue to my neighbour . . .
  to be able to say 'Amen' to God's will for me . . .
  to learn the secrets of the good life to which I am called.

But by God's grace I am what I am . . . his grace is sufficient for me . . . he never allows me to be tempted beyond my strength . . . he offers me unbounded grace, real freedom, strength and companionship.

Like Mary I am invited to bring forth Christ to the world . . . to share God's life . . . to be with him . . . to live as from the beginning he meant me to live.

And all is gift.

> 'Grace has brought me safe thus far,
> and grace will lead me home.'

OUR LADY, QUEEN OF HEAVEN

Near the cross of Jesus stood his mother. Seeing his mother and the disciple he loved standing near by, Jesus said to his mother, 'Woman, this is your son'. Then to the disciple he said, 'This is your mother'. And from that moment the disciple made a place for her in his home.

After that I saw a huge number, impossible to count, of people from every nation, race, tribe and language; they were standing in front of the throne and in front of the Lamb, dressed in white robes and holding palms in their hands. They shouted aloud, 'Victory to our God, who sits on the throne, and to the Lamb!' And all the angels who were standing in a circle round the throne prostrated themselves before the throne, and touched the ground with their foreheads, worshipping God with these words, 'Amen. Praise and glory and wisdom and thanksgiving and honour and power and strength to our God for ever and ever. Amen.' John 19: 25–27; Revelation 7: 9–12

The picture I may have of heaven need not bother me. I know I cannot even begin to imagine it and that no language can describe it for me. It is enough to appreciate the promise of the past and the reality of present hope.

The past is made by those who have gone before,
the great men and women who lived before Christ, in hope for his coming . . .
the mother of Christ, who was blessed because she believed in God's promise . . .
the apostles and disciples of Jesus, who came to believe that he was the Promised One . . .
the Christian saints, who have heard the Word of God and kept it . . .
the men and women of good will, who have searched for what is right and good and have found God.

To these, 'a number impossible to count', the risen Lord has already said: 'Come you blessed of my Father, into the kingdom prepared for you from the foundation of the world.' The word of God was sown in them and they brought forth good fruit.

Mary is their queen,
  the mother who belongs to all, because she gave her Son to the world . . .
  the daughter who gives courage to all, because of God's faithfulness to her . . .
  the virgin who gives hope to all, because of the fruitfulness of her poverty . . .
  the woman who brings comfort to all, because she believed and was saved . . .

What is my present hope?
  that God is with me, cares for me, guides me, loves me, and asks me to make my home with him . . .
  that he has given me, for the time being, charge of the world he made, to help me grow in wisdom and grace . . .
  that he has placed me in a world peopled by other men and women, my brothers and sisters, so that together we may love and serve him . . .
  that his friends who have lived in this world before me, among them especially Mary the mother of God, are my friends . . .
  that together we belong to God and to one another, and are in communion of mind, heart and soul . . .
With such a hope, I am indeed greatly blessed.

'Pray for me, a sinner,
now and at the hour of my death. Amen.'

A Meditation on the Beatitudes

'Be perfect
as your heavenly Father is perfect.'

Lord I hear you say,
'Be perfect as your heavenly Father is perfect',
and I am afraid.
I cannot do what you ask;
you don't expect me to be like God himself?
You know, Lord, that I can never be perfect.
Why do you ask me then even to try?

Perhaps you can't be perfect yet,
but you can always grow.
So set your sights high,
don't refuse to walk a bit further,
or say you have no more to give.

Never be anxious about your weaknesses;
always know that I will give you strength;
try to forgive even those who don't forgive you;
learn what it is to be free;
try not to think evil of others;
be compassionate towards your fellow-men;
be generous and unstinted in your love;
live from moment to moment
without worrying about tomorrow.

You can always walk this step,
and this step is the only one that matters.
To be perfect is not to have achieved all,
but to put no limits to your giving,
to draw no horizon to what is possible,
never to say 'Thus far and no further'.

If you can become like that
you will learn what it is to be like God.

So here is a pattern for your living
– your generous living –
that will bring you true and lasting happiness:

> Blessed are the poor in spirit,
> for theirs is the kingdom of heaven.
>
> Blessed are those who mourn,
> for they shall be comforted.
>
> Blessed are the meek,
> for they shall inherit the earth.
>
> Blessed are those who hunger and thirst for righteousness,
> for they shall be satisfied.
>
> Blessed are the merciful,
> for they shall obtain mercy.
>
> Blessed are the pure in heart,
> for they shall see God.
>
> Blessed are the peacemakers,
> for they shall be called sons of God.
>
> Blessed are those who are persecuted for righteousness' sake,
> for theirs is the kingdom of heaven.

Matthew 5: 2–10

Help me, Lord, to accept this demanding law,
that completes the law of Sinai.
Help me not to be angry with my brother,
not to lust with my mind and heart after another,
to speak the truth,
to be honest and sincere,
to offer good in return for evil,
to give to those who ask,
to trust in your goodness and care,
and to praise and thank you always. Amen.

**'Blessed are the poor in spirit,
for theirs is the kingdom of heaven.'**

There are times, Lord, when I know how poor I really am.
I know that without you I have nothing and I am nothing,
and I am happy in this knowledge.
But these times are rare.
More often, in my pride, I try to live alone –
I forget you and ignore my friends.

Even if you forget me,
I shall never forget you,
because I love you
as tenderly as a mother loves her child.
To be poor is just to let me be with you,
to empty yourself of the junk,
so that I have room in your life.
I promise that you will never then be in need
of the things that matter.
Learn to be content with who you are,
to be able to live with your failings,
to be glad about your strengths,
to rejoice in the goodness of others.
This is humility,
this is poverty.
Be like the child
who is generous in giving and receiving,
who is glad to be everyone's friend.
Poverty is a good platform for friendship.

Lord, what of the good things of life,
of food and drink, of money, security and property?
How can I have these
and still deserve the reward of the poor?

These are gifts,
and every good gift comes from me.
It is how you use them that is important –
do you use them for yourself or for others?
Accept the things of creation
and the work of human hands
gladly and responsibly.
Be honest,
share with those in need,
give generously and without anxiety.
Give of yourself,
your time, your skill, your enthusiasm,
your kindness, your forgiveness, your compassion.
Let go, empty yourself, surrender yourself to me,
then surely you will discover one day
the pearl of great price,
and will be at peace.

Lord, if at times I try to serve two masters,
be patient with me.
Teach me to recognise what is of real value
and not to worry about success, praise or material reward.
Plant in me the seed of poverty
so that one day I may hear your call
to leave all things and follow you. Amen.

'Blessed are those who mourn,
for they shall be comforted.'

I'm not sure, Lord,
whether my sadness is true mourning,
or just self-pity and depression.
I'm ashamed of my failures,
scared of being hurt,
afraid that I'll be punished for my sins,
overwhelmed when I realise what you are asking of
  me.

I was afraid too, you know.
It's human to be scared or overwhelmed,
but try not to be afraid of being human,
and remember always that you are loved
with a tremendous love.
The things that worry you
– your shame, self-anger and fear –
are only dangerous if that is where you stop.
I'm asking you to look beyond yourself
towards God, your Father, who loves you
and asks for your love and trust;
and towards the whole company of your fellow men
  and women
with their problems and anxieties –
they too ask for your love and trust.
Love God and love your neighbour as yourself.

Mourn for your sinfulness and failure
because you have been less than you are capable of
  being,
less than what God has called you to be,
and so have weakened the bond of brotherhood.
Your generous, unselfish sorrow,
that accepts responsibility
and seeks forgiveness from your Father
and from your brethren,
will indeed be comforted.

No one can refuse unselfish sorrow.

Mourn, too, with those who suffer:
with the sick, the lonely and depressed,
with the anxious and those who have no friends,
with the apparent failures of the world.
Be aware of them, care for them as best you can,
suffer with them, pray with them, weep with them.
Such real compassion brings its own reward,
of acceptance, trust and healing.
Give, and there will be gifts for you:
a full measure,
pressed down, shaken together, and running over,
will be poured into your lap;
because the amount you measure out
is the amount you will be given back.

Lord, help me to see myself
as a true member of your family,
and to know that others depend on me
as I do on them.
Bring me to a self-forgetful sorrow,
and to an unsparing compassion,
so that in learning to mourn
I may discover the comfort of your presence. Amen.

'Blessed are the meek
for they shall inherit the earth.'

Meek, Lord? What does it mean?

If you think of those who aren't meek
you'll see its meaning clearly enough.
The sharp person who trades in unkind words;
the perfectionist who finds fault in everything;
the boaster who never listens to others;
the jealous man who is afraid of your cleverness;
the authoritarian who plays everything by the rule
book;
the older person who damps the fire of your
enthusiasm;
the younger person who is impatient of your
slowness.
These sad people inherit bitterness, loneliness
and fear;
they stand on their own platform and isolate
themselves from others.

To be meek is to have discovered a quiet strength.
Learn of me for I am meek and humble of heart.

Tame yourself,
find the balance of your life,
look for the strength of self-control.
Know that anger can be a gift –
not the violence of unbridled and selfish passion,
but the force that impels you to right what is wrong.

If you are corrected for wrong-doing
accept the reproach without seeking to justify
yourself;
do not look for revenge;
be courteous towards your accusers.

Use the power you have
to set people free, and not to enslave;

blow gently on the smouldering flax;
be ready with praise and speak generously of others.

Listen sympathetically to excuses;
accept an apology unhesitatingly;
try to understand the other person's feelings;
be gentle towards those who are fearful;
act always with feeling care.

Appreciate the idealism of the young;
heed the wisdom of the old;
be patient with young and old alike;
listen attentively to authority.

Tamed by God,
you will inherit a world of peace,
where nothing can harm you,
and every man is your friend.

Lord, forgive me for my unkindness –
for the harsh and thoughtless things I do and say.
Give me the grace of self-control
and the strength to be gentle,
so that, learning to be meek and humble of heart,
I may be a friend to the friendless
and a support for the weak. Amen.

'Blessed are those who hunger and thirst for righteousness,
for they shall be satisfied.'

Lord, I do care about justice,
and try to act justly towards others.
I'm honest about money, and usually tell the truth;
I give a certain amount to charity.
I want people to be free and to be fully alive.
I get angry when I read of torture and cruelty,
and I deplore the dishonesty and callousness I see in the world.
Then I remember the parable about the pharisee and the publican,
and I wonder . . .

It is good to care about justice
and to work in whatever way you can
to bring greater freedom to the world.
But the justice I want you to practise and proclaim
is something deeper than you may yet have discovered.
The just man is the one who is at rights with God and men.
He knows that God loves him
and is always beckoning him to come closer;
he lives with God as with a familiar friend,
confident that love covers a multitude of sins;
he knows that God loved the world so much
that he sent his only Son,
so that all who believe in him would be saved.
He has learned, too, to love his enemy;
he offers the wicked man no resistance;
he is quick to forgive those who have hurt him;
he gives to those who ask, and lends without question.
He has set his heart on the things of God,
content that God's gifts will bring him deep happiness.

The grace you need to pray for
is not just to care about justice,
but to be able to hunger and thirst for what is right,
to be urgent, anxious and aching to be made right by God,
to be willing to spend yourself utterly in the quest for righteousness.
It is the grace to speak freely with outcasts without shame,
to be prepared to see the good of others, whoever they may be,
to have the courage to be thought a fool for my sake,
to have a heart big enough to contain the world.

Your search for justice is your search for God.
Ask, and it will be given to you;
search, and you will find;
knock, and the door will be opened to you.

Be sure that you will have your fill:
in justifying others you yourself will be justified;
by easing another's burden you will be made free;
in leading your friend to God your search will be satisfied.

Lord, you know how half-hearted I am in my search,
and how often I blind myself to what is truly right.
Forgive my lack of urgency and eagerness.
Set me on fire with your Spirit,
show me the path of justice,
and give me the vision and courage to live as your disciple. Amen.

**'Blessed are the merciful,
for they shall obtain mercy.'**

Have I ever the chance, Lord, to be merciful?
Isn't this something for people with authority,
like judges, magistrates, the police, teachers, or
employers?
I don't have power over others,
so how can I show mercy?

You often ask for mercy:
you pray, 'Lord, have mercy';
but do you realise what you are asking for?
It should be more than a plea not to be punished,
or for the scales of justice to be balanced in your
favour.
God is not a magistrate or an employer
who has to apply the law rigorously
and treat everyone according to what they deserve.
He is your Father.
He is full of compassion and love,
and he has made a promise with you
that come what may he will never disown you.
He will not forget you or leave you;
he will always be faithful and steadfast.
This is his mercy –
his promise to reach out to poor, weak, and sinful
men,
so that with his free gift they may live.
Your prayer for mercy is a reminder to God
for him to fulfill his promise to you –
to be compassionate, patient, forgiving, loving
towards you.

Mercy is a truly godly quality.
It enriches the bond between you and your friends –
and enemies.
If you would be great, practise mercy towards others.

Remember the parable about the unforgiving debtor,
who, though his own huge debt was cancelled,
demanded payment from his fellow-worker –
and learn to forgive as often as you are injured.

Read the story of the latecomers to the vineyard,
who, because of the generosity of their employer,
were paid the same wages as the rest –
and discover the love that exceeds justice.

Recall the wounded man who, ignored by his friends,
was cared for by his enemy, the Samaritan –
and know that it is in deeds that mercy is shown.

In all your dealings with others,
whether as one in authority or not,
be aware of them as your companions in the Lord;
understand their strengths and weaknesses, their burdens and gifts;
be tolerant of their failures
as you would want them to be tolerant of yours.
Your trust in them will help them trust in you;
your faithfulness to them will encourage them to love.

Your mercy will be twice blessed:
'It blesseth him that gives, and him that takes.'

Lord, be merciful to me a sinner!
Through the experience of your mercy to me
may my love for others become more generous.
May it be a practical love that responds to what is needed,
a forgiving love that does not impose conditions,
and an understanding love that sustains the weary soul. Amen.

**'Blessed are the pure in heart,
for they shall see God.'**

Lord, you search me and you know me,
you know my deepest thoughts and feelings.
So often I do those things I don't want to do,
and fail to do what in my inmost heart I eagerly desire.
I pray for purity of mind and heart and body,
yet my prayer seems unanswered.
Shall I ever see God face to face?

Your cross, which you cannot escape, is yourself.
Accept this burden gratefully and willingly,
and realise that it is a blessing for you
to be this woman or this man.
Like any cross you may want to shrug it off at times;
then come to me and you will find rest for your soul.
If you would be my disciple you must bear with
yourself.
I shall not let you be tried beyond your strength.

The attraction you have for others and they for you
is something to praise God for,
not to be ashamed or frightened of.
See in it a source of your growth,
and not a threat to your immortality.

Take courage.
What is in your heart is what is most important.
It is from the heart that evil comes,
and if your heart is pure
and the spirit is willing,
then even if the flesh is weak
you shall find forgiveness and hope.

Learn, if you can, from the purity of the child.
There is in him a simplicity and directness
that dissolves all prejudice and anger.
His innocence is a light
that the darkness cannot overpower.

His friendship is for everyone.
His thoughts go with uncomplicated ease
to the heart of the problem.
He is pure, untouched by evil, unadulterated.

Do not judge yourself too harshly.
Strive to be simple and sincere.
Remember the importance of a humble and contrite heart.
Do not be anxious about your motives,
but do straightforwardly what you see to be right.

One day your cross will be mounted like mine on Calvary,
so that through that final death
you may take up your new life with God.
Then you will know him face to face
and the purity of your heart will at last triumph
over the weakness of your body.
I am the resurrection and the life;
he who believes in me will have eternal life.

Lord, when my eyes are blinded
and my ears are deafened by false attractions,
keep my heart fixed on you.
Help me to find again the sincerity and simplicity
that leads direct to you,
the object of my real desire. Amen.

**'Blessed are the peacemakers,
for they shall be called sons of God.'**

Lord, you can't open a newspaper or listen to the news
without learning of some new attack on peace.
There's everything from the threat of nuclear war
to statistics on divorce.
How does a follower of yours
even begin to struggle against these evils?

Do you believe that true peace is possible,
or do you in your heart of hearts
think that this is an impossible dream?

There is only one road to peace,
and that is for you to be at peace in yourself
and with your fellow men and women.
Love your neighbour as yourself.
Love your enemy,
do good to those who insult you,
pray for those who persecute and caluminate you.

I came to bring peace.
My work was to build bridges between people,
and to span the gulf between man and God.
It meant trying to break the barriers of prejudice,
healing those who were sick in body, mind and soul,
helping people to realise that they could be free.
If you want to be my disciple
this is your work too.

Your personal peace will come with the knowledge
that you are truly forgiven and redeemed.
My peace I leave you, my peace I give you;
a peace that is more than the ending of conflict,
rather the meeting of minds and hearts
that marks the beginning of reconciliation and
contentment.
Your certainty that you are safe in God's hands

is what gives you the authority and power to make
peace.

It will give you the courage to be uncompromising
in confronting violence and slavery.
It will show you the gentleness needed
in healing those hurt by evil.
It will bring you the wisdom and skill
to temper anger and remove suspicion.

You may not sway the world,
remove the threat of war,
decrease the crime rate,
or make marriage more stable.
But be sure that by your actions for peace
the world is thereby blessed.
Without your tears the ocean is the poorer.

If you make peace even in small things,
you are my brother or sister,
and will share my inheritance with the Father.

Lord, give me the strength, confidence and patience
to work for a true and lasting peace.
May I find peace in my own heart,
and bring your peace to family, friends and fellow-
workers.
Help me to do the small things well
so that the greater may follow,
for your sake and for the world. Amen.

'Blessed are those who are persecuted for
righteousness' sake,
for theirs is the kingdom of heaven.'

I admire the martyrs, Lord, and deeply respect them,
but I'm not that sort of person.
I don't think I'd stand up to persecution,
and in any case I don't really do anything
that people would want to attack me for.

Has anyone ever derided your faith,
attacked your stand for Christian morality,
or smiled at your praying?
Do you ever deny yourself something on my account,
suffer because men pass me by,
or accept the pain of cross-bearing?
If you are faithful in these things
you are already a witness to my name,
and in your witnessing you are a martyr.

If you live up to your Christian calling
you are certain, sooner or later, to be persecuted.
As my disciple you will slowly learn to be different,
to be a sign of contradiction to those
who worship other gods.
Your standards will rebuke the world,
so that your own people will disown you.
Even by your silence you will confront others
and risk their anger and contempt.
You will be in the world, but not of it.

As a member of my own Body
I invite you to speak on my behalf –
boldly, in season and out of season, to prophesy.
I ask you to take your part, by word and action,
in preaching the truth my Father has revealed,
to a world that is hungry for truth.

Embrace this truth yourself;
live according to the truth;

proclaim the truth with conviction;
share the truth willingly.
You can be confident, for I am with you.
I shall send you the Spirit of truth
who will teach you all things
and fill you with the fire of his love.
And the truth will set you free.

When they persecute you,
teach them to love,
for perfect love casts out fear;
and forgive them,
for they know not what they do.

Rejoice and be glad,
for the suffering of the saints brings life to a fallen world.
Your reward will be great in heaven.

Lord, I pray for the grace to become a Christian.
Teach me how to live a gospel life:
help me always to stand up for the truth,
and never to condone a lie by my inaction.
May I learn to suffer gladly for bearing your name,
so that the world may know that you have sent me,
and that your word is true. Amen.

A Meditation on the Way of the Cross

THE FIRST STATION

Jesus is condemned to death

The play-acting that has been taking place is a perfect example of the weak-minded judge.

Pilate is frightened –
of the Jews, of Caesar, of Christ.

The hand-washing is the crowning sign
of his weakness.

He had power, but would have had no power at all
were it not given from above.

'Judge not and you shall not be judged.'

Yet I often judge others . . .
sometimes needlessly and rashly.

Is it ever for me to judge another man . . .
or his motives?

Can I ever do so rightly?

Perhaps sometimes I have to make a judgement.

Then, Lord, let me do so with real justice,
and with mercy.

Let my motive always be love . . .
love of God and neighbour and not of self.

Help me always to judge others
as I would have them judge me.

Teach me to judge others
as I would have you judge me.

THE SECOND STATION

Jesus takes up his cross

A cross is synonymous in our language with a burden . . . something heavy, unwieldly, unwanted.

Jesus carrying his cross has made the cross a symbol of victory.

It has become the sign in which we conquer.

We need not think of it as a burden –
'my yoke is sweet, my burden light'.

What is my cross?

It is myself with all my failings, imperfections, eccentricities.

It is my fears . . .
the fear of facing up to my responsibilities . . .
the fear of boredom with my daily routine . . .
the fear of being found out . . .
the fear of what other people think of me . . .
the fear of loneliness . . .
the fear of failure.

'Take up your cross daily, and come follow me.'

Jesus, I am lumbered with myself . . . help me to find my feet.

THE THIRD STATION

Jesus falls the first time

It is incredible that Jesus Christ, God made man,
should fall down.

We have to remind ourselves that he was man,
'Like us in all things except sin.'

He was born . . . was nursed like any other baby . . .
he grew up, and advanced 'in wisdom and knowledge
and grace before God and man.'

He was subject to the same laws of nature
as ourselves.

He was a man . . . as physically weak as all men
are . . . he knew his weakness: 'My Father, if it
be possible, let this cup pass from me . . .'

Do I know my weakness?

Is it part of my trouble that I think I'm stronger
than I really am?

Am I too impatient in my passage towards God?

Do I stumble through over-confidence?

Help me to know my weakness, Lord, so that I can
overcome the petty faults which keep me from you . . .
my thoughtlessness towards others . . .
my carelessness in prayer . . .
my obstinacy in holding to my own opinion . . .
my impatience and irritability.

Help me, Jesus, to learn by my mistakes, and always
to lean on you.

THE FOURTH STATION

Jesus meets his blessed mother

Can we really imagine this?

The summit of a mother's selflessness –
the giving of her son.

Even if she knew all that was involved it was still a loss . . .
an inexpressible anguish . . .
a suffering with him in perfect sympathy . . .
a weight of sadness that there was so little she could do to help . . .
a contentment that she could be with him and comfort him.

Isn't this often a mother's and a father's sorrow?
The loss, for a time, of their children?

Isn't it, too, a child's sorrow?
To be cut off from his parents by misunder-
standing . . . a desire for freedom from control . . .
loneliness . . . a feeling of being unwanted?

Young people have their own cross to carry
to the top of their own Calvary.

On the way they need the affection, sympathy, security of their family –
who perhaps, like Mary, can do so little to help.

Help me, Mary, to take my cue from you . . .
to bear, if need be, the sight of my children leaving
me . . . to be with them when I'm needed . . .
to hide from them my own sadness.

Help me, Jesus, to be understanding with my
parents, and to let them help me.

THE FIFTH STATION

Simon of Cyrene helps Jesus to carry his cross

What sort of a man was Simon . . . what did he do for a living . . . why was he in Jerusalem . . . why was he watching this sordid procession?

He was probably a very ordinary person like you or me . . . just in from the country for a day or two . . . eager to see the city sights . . . inquisitive for cheap entertainment.

Then he was hauled out from the crowd and forced to take part in it all.

How did he react?

Surely he was first of all angry and afraid.

This is so often my reaction when I'm pilloried in any way – anger and fear.

Angry that someone has doubted my word . . .
afraid that perhaps I'm not right after all.

Angry because my little pedestal has been upset . . .
afraid that I won't be able to get back on it again.

Angry with the foolishness of others who don't or won't hold the same view as me . . .
afraid that I may be made to look more foolish than them.

Help me, Lord Jesus, to master my fear and anger, which so often stems from pride and self-love.

Help me to be at peace with myself, following in your footsteps.

THE SIXTH STATION

Veronica wipes the face of Jesus

This is a simple act of charity . . .
but splendidly heroic and uniquely rewarded.

I don't have the chance to perform acts like that . . .
indeed, I'm foolish if I think I can.

This is part of my trouble –
I day-dream all the time . . .

I wonder what I would have done . . .
would I have behaved like Veronica . . .
or Simon . . .
or Peter . . .
or Judas . . .

But such wondering is fruitless.

All I need to ask is whether I do, here and now,
behave like Veronica.

If I do, the reward is the same . . .
I receive the imprint of Christ on my life.

'Put on then, as God's chosen ones, holy and beloved, compassion . . . kindness . . . lowliness . . . meekness . . . patience . . . forbearing one another . . . forgiving each other.'

'Above all these put on love, which binds everything together in perfect harmony.'

This is both the reward of our charity
and its cause.

THE SEVENTH STATION

Jesus falls the second time

In the garden Jesus prayed:

'My Father, if it be possible, let this cup pass from me;
nevertheless, not as I will, but as thou wilt.'

On the cross he said:

'My God, my God, why hast thou forsaken me?'

Did Jesus have difficulty on the way of the cross?
We take for granted, almost, his perseverance . . .
his trust in his heavenly Father.
But this was genuine perseverance, genuine trust.

There is nothing sham in the humanity of Christ.

My way of the cross is pretty easy by comparison.
Yet I, too, need trust and the grace of perseverance . . .
and especially in the sacrament of penance.

My sins are so routine . . .
I have to confess the same ones again and again . . .
maybe I can take comfort in this . . .
perhaps I'm getting no worse.

I must learn to persevere in my sorrow . . .
to show, by my actions, that my sorrow is real . . .
never to let my conscience become calloused . . .
never to become oblivious to a fault, however slight it seems to be . . .
never to stop trying.

I must learn to trust more completely in God . . .
to have an unwearied hope that in the end, like Christ, I shall overcome.
After all, God has promised me just that.

THE EIGHTH STATION

The women of Jerusalem mourn for Jesus

These were kind people who were genuinely sad to see such suffering. But in spite of their sincerity and kindness they missed the point. 'Was it not necessary that the Christ should suffer these things and enter into his glory?'

Do I mourn about the right things?

'Woe upon you who laugh now,
you shall mourn and weep.'
'Blessed are you who weep now,
you will laugh for joy.'

There is so much false joy in the world –
escapism . . . ridicule . . . irony . . . facetiousness . . .
the degrading of human virtue . . . mockery . . .
pleasure seeking.

This is only a preparation for tears.

Sorrow can lead to misery . . . to bitterness . . .
to despair . . . to frustration . . .
to rejection of the truth.

This sorrow is without faith . . . or hope . . .
or charity.

In our sorrow we can always come to God . . . 'You who weep now come to this God, for he is weeping.' By our tears we make up what is lacking in the sorrows of Christ. This can be the true sorrow that leads us to joy. The joy that we are part of God's plan, that we can share in the Incarnation . . . in the Redemption.

Joy is the keynote of Christian spirituality. The gospel is the good news of great joy. The origin of our joy is the Incarnation . . . 'the God who became man, that man might become God.'

THE NINTH STATION

Jesus falls the third time

We can scarcely blame the onlookers if they failed to see this as a triumphal journey. The psalmist's description is accurate enough –

'I am a worm and not a man,
  the scorn of men and despised of the people.
I am poured out like water,
  and all my bones are disjointed.
My heart has become like wax,
  melting away within my breast.
My throat is dried up like a potsherd,
  my tongue cleaves to my jaws,
  and in the dust of death you have laid me.'

A description, in its way, of me.
Weak of will . . .
lax of conscience . . .
dry of love.
In such a state I deserve to be despised.

I need both goading and encouraging.

You speak to me, Lord, when I pray –
encourage me to listen to you patiently.

You speak to me, Lord, when I am reading or listening to a sermon –
encourage me to listen humbly . . . intelligently . . . without undue criticism. Unless I become as a little child, I shall not enter into the kingdom of heaven.

Lord, goad me to perfection.

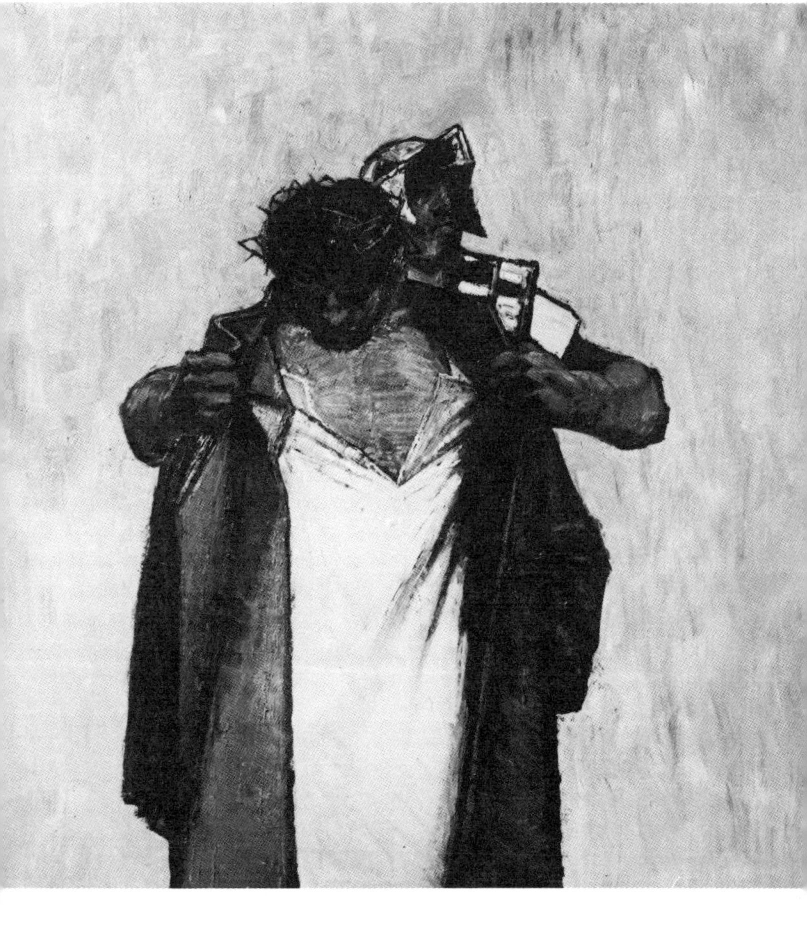

THE TENTH STATION

Jesus is stripped of his clothes

By way of humiliation this was the last straw.

> 'Who, though he was in the form of God,
> did not count equality with God a thing to be grasped,
> but emptied himself,
> taking the form of a servant,
> being born in the likeness of men.
>
> And being found in human form,
> he humbled himself,
> and became obedient unto death,
> even death on a cross.'

He did not prize his possessions,
neither those due to him as God . . .
nor those due to him as man.

He had no home . . .
was often hungry and thirsty . . .
was born in poverty . . . and died in poverty.

I like to pretend to myself that I am poor in spirit.
But sometimes I find myself terribly concerned
about trivialities –
Can I afford a new fridge? . . . a new car? . . . a new suit? . . .
Should I take out another insurance policy? . . .
Will I get a rise next week . . . month . . . year?

I know well enough that I'm not a lily of the field and that I must toil and spin, but I wonder whether I'm often over-concerned about taking care for tomorrow?

Help me, Lord Jesus, to be genuinely poor in spirit . . . to find a proper balance between caution and recklessness . . . to deepen my understanding of Providence.

THE ELEVENTH STATION

Jesus is nailed to the cross

It is the sheer, unmitigated cruelty of it which disgusts us first of all. It seems unbelievable that man, created in the image and likeness of God, should be able to sink to such depths.
We call such acts barbaric, inhuman.

Cruelty survives today on the grand scale –
the concentration camps . . .
the violence of modern crime . . .
the savage cruelty of some towards their children.

With me it may be a question of motes and beams turned back to front. I am so scandalised by the viciousness of some, that I scarcely notice the speck of inhumanity in myself –
my barbed wit . . .
my lack of charity towards motorists or pedestrians . . .
my ignoring of those I don't want to like . . .
my willingness to gossip and say something hurtful . . .
my condescension towards those more ignorant than myself . . .
my impatience with those younger – or older – than myself . . .

Pinpricks – which beside Christ's wounds are as nothing.
But these are my faults,
for which I am answerable.

Help me, Jesus, to heal the wounds caused by hate, and to show to all men the love you have shown to me.

'Forgive us our trespasses as we forgive those who trespass against us.'

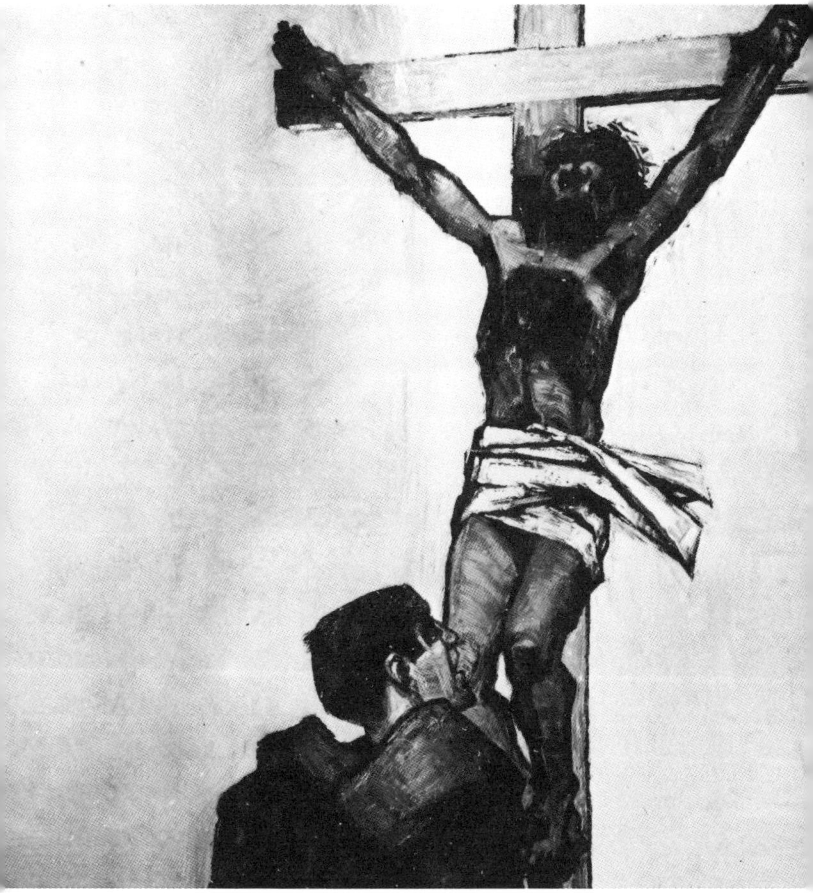

THE TWELFTH STATION

Jesus dies on the cross

'It was about the sixth hour, and there was darkness over the whole land until the ninth hour, while the sun's light failed; and the curtain of the temple was torn in two. Then Jesus, crying out with a loud voice, said, "Father, into thy hands I commend my spirit!" And having said this he breathed his last.'

> 'Without beauty, without majesty (we saw him),
> no looks to attract our eyes;
> a thing despised and rejected by men,
> a man of sorrows and familiar with suffering.
> And yet ours were the sufferings he bore,
> ours the sorrows he carried.'

'Greater love has no man than this,
that a man lay down his life for his friends.'

> 'I am the Lord your God . . . your Saviour . . .
> you are precious in my eyes . . . and I love you . . .
>
> Fear not, for I am with you . . .
> you are my witnesses . . .
> my chosen people . . .
> the people whom I formed for myself . . .
>
> Turn to me and be saved, for I am God . . .
> Return to me, for I have redeemed you.'

'And I, when I am lifted up from the earth,
will draw all men to myself.'

'Unless a grain of wheat falls into the earth and dies,
it remains alone; but if it dies, it bears much fruit.'

THE THIRTEENTH STATION

Jesus is taken down from the cross

'Like us in all things except sin'.

The dead body of Jesus. It is hard to take this in . . . that Jesus really died . . . that his body became a lifeless thing . . . an empty shell.

If we have seen death we know how unreal a dead body looks. It is so obviously empty . . . incomplete . . . utterly different from what it was a few moments before.

And yet, 'Truly this was the Son of God.'

I wouldn't be human if I were entirely unafraid of death.

The saint may say, 'I desire to be dissolved and to be with Christ';
but if I say this, the words are a little hollow.

Yet in spite of my natural human fear,
I have hope . . .
Christ has been there before me.

My only wish is that when God calls me
I shall be able to say, like Christ,
'It is finished, the work you gave me is done.'

Help me, Lord Jesus, to approach death unafraid,
confident that I have tried to do your will.

THE FOURTEENTH STATION

Jesus is placed in the tomb

'He descended into hell. The third day he rose again from the dead. He ascended into heaven and sits on the right hand of God the almighty Father . . .' continually interceding on our behalf.

The grave is only a passing resting place . . .
for us as for Christ.

The life, death, resurrection and ascension of Jesus Christ is the promise for us of eternal life.

We are one body with Christ –
we are no longer alone in our pursuit for God . . .
we go with Christ . . .
we go as other Christs . . .

We share each other's blessings and burdens –
forgetful of self . . .
filled with the same hope . . .
fired with the same faith . . .
united in the same love for each other and for God.

I pray that in my life I may mirror Christ –
that I may truly die to sin . . .
that I may make my daily round my daily prayer . . .
that by my love I may lead others to Christ . . .
that in my God-given vocation I may be all things to all men.

I know that my Redeemer lives, and that through him, with him and in him, all of us shall find life.

An Examination of Conscience

Every now and then it is valuable for us to pause and look at ourselves, so as to see how we are living. It may be helpful to do this by reflecting on our Lord's teaching – for instance, the Beatitudes, one of the parables, or the account of the Last Judgement. Tradition suggests that the Portrait of Love given by St Paul (1 Corinthians 13: 4–13) is a description of Jesus himself. So it is given here as a background against which we may see ourselves. If it is used as part of a night prayer, it may well be enough to choose one phrase only to think about.

'Love is always patient and kind' . . .

Am I patient with myself?
Do I expect too much of myself?
Do I get angry with myself when I fail?

> Am I impatient in prayer?
> Do I stop praying if I don't get quick results?
> Do I remember to pray for others?

Am I patient with others?
Do I get irritable at other people's failures or weaknesses or eccentricities, or if they are less quick or clever than me?

Am I patient and kind with children, the elderly and sick?
Am I patient with those who work with me or for me?
Do I listen patiently to those in authority?

Am I gentle and kind in my speech?
Do I speak well of others?
Do I act kindly towards those in a less privileged position than me?

. . . 'it is never jealous, boastful or conceited' . . .

Am I jealous of someone else's good fortune, or success?
Do I try to keep up with my next door neighbour?
Do I drive my children (or others) so that I can boast of them?

Am I affronted if others don't live up to my expectations?
Do I expect more of others than I do of myself?
Do I criticise others so that they lose confidence in themselves?

Am I complacent about myself?
Am I hypocritical in the way I live?
Do I keep on comparing myself with others?

Do I look for praise from others?
Am I slow to thank, to encourage or to praise?
Do I bore others by talking about myself?

Do I bother to listen to others?
Am I slow to apologise or to admit my faults?
Do I show my gratitude to God and my fellow men for all they do for me?

... 'it is never rude or selfish' ...

Do I treat others with the respect due to them as persons?
Am I chaste in my relationships with others?
Do I sin against purity in mind or action?

Does my language reflect my human dignity?
Am I ever arrogant, obstinate or overbearing?
Does my chattering prevent others from speaking?

Do I insist on what I want before thinking about others?
Do I inconvenience others by my selfish use of transistor, TV or record player?
Do I consider the effect that my actions will have on others?

Do I take a genuine interest in the needs of the Third World?
Is my attitude to material things determined by selfish motives?
Do I use my own and other people's property with due care?

Do I ever deliberately hurt another?
Do I seek for pleasure at the expense of others?
Does my selfishness ever lead me to ignore God?

. . . 'it does not take offence, and is not resentful' . . .

Am I touchy about my rights?
Am I prepared to accept criticism?
Do I feel slighted if others are preferred to me?

How do I react to my failures?
How do I respond if I am unjustly treated or misunderstood?
Am I willing to accept injustice as Christ did, with meekness?

What is my attitude to law; do I ignore it if it inconveniences me?
Do I impose laws on others that I am not prepared to keep myself?
Do I act on what Christ said: 'If you love me you will keep my commandments'?

Do I forgive those who sin against me?
Do I ask forgiveness from those whom I have sinned against?
Am I resentful at the way God treats me?

Do I drive others to resentment by harshness, unreasonableness, thoughtlessness, or selfishness?
Am I resentful of my own weaknesses?
Do I resent my dependence on others and on God?

. . . 'Love delights in truth' . . .

Am I a truthful person?
Do I try to grow in the understanding of truth?
Do I pray for God's Spirit of truth in my life?

Do I repeat what I hear without bothering to verify its truth or falsity?
Do I gossip, or spread rumours, or scandal?
Do I hide or distort truth by my speech, my actions or my silence?

Do I respect those who sincerely hold different beliefs to mine?
Do I try to understand the beliefs of others?
Do I allow others freedom to accept truth, or do I put unjust pressures on them?

Do I witness by word and example to the truth of the Gospel?
As a teacher do I take the trouble to learn?
Do I ever compromise the truth for fear of what others may think?

Is my life a true reflection of my beliefs?
Do I try to share my vision of truth with others?
Do I look and listen for God in my life?

. . . 'it is always ready to excuse, to trust, to hope' . . .

Do I take Christ's advice: 'Judge not and you shall not be judged'?
Am I quicker to judge others than I am to judge myself?
Do I try to understand the actions of others?

Do I make excuses for myself when I sin?
Am I able to forgive myself?
Do I have a firm hope that God will give me his grace?

Am I ready to accept others whatever their faults?
Am I willing to trust others even when they let me down?
Do I help others to grow and to hope by putting my trust in them?

Do I see justice and mercy as being in conflict?
Am I rigid in my application of the law?
Am I ready to be generous in forgiving?

Do I accept that I shall not be tried beyond my strength?